The Call of the Psalms:
A Spiritual Companion for Busy People

by Rev. Joanna J. Seibert, M. D.

Deacon, Trinity Episcopal Cathedral,
Little Rock, Arkansas
Former Director of Radiology,
Arkansas Children's Hospital
Professor of Radiology and Pediatrics,
University of Arkansas for Medical Sciences

Temenos Publishing ~ Little Rock, Arkansas

Cover art by Mitchell Crisp
Cover photo by Joanna J. Seibert from the Chapel of the Good Shepherd at the National Cathedral in Washington, D.C.

A portion of the proceeds from the sale of
The Call of the Psalms: A Spiritual Companion for Busy People
will go to The Cathedral School in Little Rock, AR

ISBN 0-9785648-7-1

*T*emenos Publishing
411 Main St.
North Little Rock, AR 72114
501-772-7602
www.temenospublishing.com

Advance Praise for *The Call of the Psalms*

"Many are deprived of entering into the treasures contained in
The Psalms perhaps through a constricted knowledge of them,
or the cursory rattling off of them that is characteristic of so
much Sunday worship. *The Call of the Psalms* provides an
effective antidote for that deprivation. As a physician, deacon,
musician, and spiritual director who is thoroughly familiar
with all sorts of physical and spiritual diseases and addictions,
Joanna Seibert's personal reflections on how The Psalms have
impacted her own self-understanding and spiritual growth is
a significant gift to all of us. Whether one is seeking to
understand and better enter into the heart of The Psalter, or
whether one is desirous of improving one conscious contact
with God, *The Call of the Psalms* is a Grace-full door to such an
adventure."

The Rt. Rev. Robert B. Hibbs
Bishop Suffragan
Episcopal Diocese of West Texas (res)

"Three of the main ingredients for spiritual growth are
honesty, open-mindedness and willingness. In her reflections
Joanna Seibert has combined liberal amounts of all three, and
the result is a concoction guaranteed to quicken the pulse of
those who journey in the Spirit. As revealed in her salutary
reflection upon authentic experience, the spiritual life
coruscates when it takes it cue from the Psalmist: affliction in
seasons of comfort and comfort for times of affliction."

The Rev. Stuart H. Hoke, ThD
Pittsboro, North Carolina

"Joanna Seibert has a real gift for telling stories that help each of us to connect with the deeper meaning behind the poetry that is contained in the Psalms. In the hands of the loving Lord who is illuminated by her words, her willingness to be really honest about who she is and the God she trusts serves as an encouragement to me to do likewise. This book is one that I will always treasure and learn from every time I read it. I trust you will also."

Eleanor Stromberger
Past President of Recovery Ministries

What readers are saying about *The Call of the Psalms:*

"I have loved reading *The Call of the Psalms.* The readings have been little moments of respite in my hectic days. I've never read the Psalms, so it was interesting to read them but even more interesting to read your comments and experiences. Through you I was able to think of how these teachings applied in my own life and recovery. My youngest sister is a traditional Catholic. Over the past few months we've been sharing feelings and concerns about our lives. I have shared these readings with her. Even though our religious views are different, this book has helped bring us even closer."

"It was nice to know that someone else actually struggles daily with some of the same issues that I do."

"The meditations always touched me in some way and were so very relevant to what was going on in my life at the moment. Thank you so much. I would definitely recommend this book to others."

"*The Call of the Psalms* has been an excellent reminder of the need to stay centered daily on what's really important."

"Daily reading *The Call of the Psalms* has helped me make it through each day."

"*The Call of the Psalms* has been a good reminder to stop and pay attention to what matters. I think you summed it all up with this: 'The world tells us to strive for success, power, accomplishments, projects, goals. The Psalms tell us to strive for our relationship with God on a daily, hourly, momentary basis.' "

"The reading today touched my heart. It was so full of wisdom and humor."

"The author's honesty and ability to put into words exact feelings that I have often moves me to tears. It is especially wonderful to identify with the feelings of jealousy, inadequacy, revenge, and injustice that she writes about in such a compelling way. She has led us on a sacred journey."

"These meditations really hit home. I never thought of God's presence in my life quite like this."

"Thank you for these words that have helped me on my journey."

"This meditation was right where I am. It brought tears to my eyes, even. I've been so angry and hurt over things in my life. While I'm trying to practice acceptance and faith and love, it's not easy. So I will try to focus on reaching out to others and see if that helps me to be grateful for what I have and what I am able to do, rather focusing on others' opinions that what I do doesn't appear to be good enough for them."

"The story about your son and his grandfather almost made me cry. It was just beautiful."

"The Psalms and the meditative responses help keep me grounded in my search for progress not perfection."

"I felt God's presence in the room of a dying soul friend just as you described with the dying young girl and her grandmother."

"Thank you for these candid writings. Everyday I get something worthwhile to think about."

"I was feeling caught up in 'busyness' this afternoon when I read the Psalm and your meditation. Thank you for the timely reminder to slow down."

"The meditation today was on target in describing depressive episodes and was very insightful about how to deal with it."

"This meditation brought back some of the painful and wonderful trips back home."

"My spiritual life also revolves around several groups. As a fellow physician, your messages are so helpful for me. I am learning that it is not really 'all about me.' "

"These meditations are an amazing gift. I share the writings with my family. They think they are so profound, yet simple, and touch us deep in our soul."

"This is the best explanation of being God centered and God directed that I have ever heard."

"Thank you for reminding me of one of my 'peak' experiences as a child at church camp."

In thanksgiving for Robert, my companion and soul-mate, in celebration of our 40 years of marriage.

The Serenity Prayer

God grant me the serenity
to accept the things I cannot change;
courage to change the things I can;
and wisdom to know the difference.

Living one day at a time;
Enjoying one moment at a time;
Accepting hardships as the pathway to peace;
Taking, as He did, this sinful world
as it is, not as I would have it;
Trusting that He will make all things right
if I surrender to His Will;
That I may be reasonably happy in this life
and supremely happy with Him
Forever in the next.
Amen.

--Reinhold Niebuhr

Preface

The Psalter has always been the well of consolation and the oasis of refreshment for the men and women of many ages, faiths, and circumstances. The full range of human emotion is caught in its songs, as is the full range of human conversation about, and toward, the divine.

But the Psalter is also known as the poor person's greatest consolation. It is known by that descriptive name, in fact, not only because of its overt or obvious content, but also because of an inherent subtlety: One must be poor in heart and spirit to drink both deeply and completely from its waters.

The Psalter requires as well that those who dare to speak of its treasures – to comment upon them, to parse them and mine them for their mysteries as well as their consolation – must likewise come on humble feet and with a heart made pure by devotion, by experience, and by a certain familiarity with sorrow and the agonies, as well as the triumphs, of our human condition.

Joanna Seibert has entered the Psalter and explicated the Psalms before, both publicly and privately. But she has never done so with as rich a result as that which she achieves here in this slender volume of narratives. 150 of them, in fact, one for each of the Psalms. She writes candidly as a Christian and without artifice, certainly, but she also writes as a healer. It is her physician-mind and worshipping heart that, in combination, make of this book a balm for the spirit and a healing draught for the soul.

Whether we read to our souls' health or to our hearts' joy makes little or no difference, however. What matters is that we read; for you and I and the world around us will all be the better for our having read and understood what treasures of the spirit there are awaiting us here.

Phyllis Tickle
The Farm in Lucy
Fifteenth Week of Pentecost, 2009

Foreword

For the faithful, this timely book inspires, promotes peace and love, and provides a path to a better, longer, and more independent life. These thoughts and verses are put together by a physician of great strength and intellect who, through faith, study, and a deep commitment to spirituality, is the finest example of the path we should all follow. Exploring these pages will do much more than merely be a way to bring you closer to your faith; these pages have the potential of providing you with a longer, more independent, healthier life with a reduced risk of many serious illnesses. The message is clear that embracing faith prolongs life, reduces disease risk, and allows those who believe to far more easily deal with serious adversities and illnesses.

It does not matter what faith you belong to, which denomination, liberal or conservative: these verses are beneficial to all. The key element of faith that links to health is being a spiritual human being. Spending time exploring the pages of this book has the potential of truly showing you the way as each page illustrates, in its own way, an element of spirituality and ways to implement the important message.

There are many elements of spirituality that link closely to health, and these should be at the front of your consciousness as you spend time, hopefully in an ideal setting, delving into the messages that Joanna Seibert brings through the unique choices she has made in putting the book together.

To be spiritual you should possess the four characteristics that each in its own way makes you a better, and remarkably healthier, person. First, you must be *good* -- meaning that you are an honest, ethical person with high integrity. Second, you must have *love and hope*. "In the end," said St. Paul, "there are only three things of value, hope, love, and faith, and of these the most important is love." Third, you must be a *giving* person. "Tsedaka" in Hebrew, "charity" in English, must be practiced every day. Volunteer 14 hours a week, and your life expectancy is prolonged by 5 years. The more you give to a good cause the longer you live. Charity is an insurance policy to a longer, better, and more complete life. And finally remember *forgiveness*, the most powerful element of the truly faithful, so difficult at times but so critical if we wish to move away from the wrong and toward the right path of peace and tranquility. Seeking redemption is the cornerstone of the growing, spiritual, and faithful human being.

Through the pages of this book you will be able to grow spiritually, achieve a higher sense of well being, and remarkably promote your health in the most powerful of ways.

David Lipschitz MD Ph.D.
Director of the Longevity Center
St. Vincent Medical Center
Little Rock AR

Introduction

The Psalms repeatedly call me to remember my connection to God who has cared for us since the beginning of time, "hiding us under the shadow of his wings" (17) or " like a weaned child" with its mother (131). When life becomes too busy, when times are difficult, when resentments overtake me, when the spiritual life is dry, I can read the Psalms during daily meditation and often find Sabbath or rest in God. I am learning the haunting call of the Psalms: the rhythm, the music, the poetry, the familiarity, the history. They call and comfort and change me as they have for so many before us. They are like the steady rhythm of the waves, coming and going, always present, sometimes pounding surf, sometimes a gentle ripple, sometimes angry, sometimes joyful, often grateful, but always a constant symbol of the rhythm of life, the difficulties of life, and the steadfast love of God. I share with you stories of a connection to God in the workplace, at home, and on retreats that have grown out of reading the Psalms. I share experiences of finding God and seeking to live a connected life.

This book contains selected verses from the 150 Psalms that can be read daily, either in the morning or at night. Following each Psalm is a story related to the Psalm and then an action to be considered. This meditative rhythm of a cycle of reading the Psalms and stories should be helpful to all persons in today's world. One of the keys to listening to God's whispers is repetition and sitting in silence.

May reading the Psalms and these stories bring you peace and strength with your walk with God. May the Psalms and the stories be a constant reminder, guidepost, and

1

roadmap for you to become the person you have been created to be. May they lead you into renewed paths of hope and knowledge and action. May they bring you the peace in your life you are seeking on this daily journey. May you know the love of a power, creator, guide, and comforter that is greater than yourself that you will often meet in community.

Joanna J. Seibert, 2009

I said to my soul, be still, and wait without hope

For hope would be hope for the wrong things; wait without love

For love would be love of the wrong thing; there is yet faith

But the faith and love and the hope are all in the waiting.

Wait without thought, for you are not ready for thought:

So the darkness shall be the light, and the stillness the dancing.

--T.S. Eliot

Psalm 1

"On his law, they meditate day and night.
They are like trees planted by streams of water,
Which yield their fruit in its season,
And their leaves do not wither."

The dreaded call comes late at night. "Your grandfather is in a coma. We think he had a stroke." In the morning I board the first plane back to my hometown of Tidewater, Virginia to visit him.

Thoughts flood my mind on the long plane ride. My grandfather was the most significant person in my growing up years. I spent every Sunday afternoon and evening with him and my grandmother. We ate the same Sunday dinner: fried chicken, green beans, potato salad, and Mabel's (my grandparents' cook) homemade pound cake. After dinner I would sit on his knee as he read me the funny papers. We all then took a short nap. I can still see him and my grandmother lying together on the small couch in their dining room/den. Then we would go to the country to his farm, walking the length of his property by the river as he told me stories about his growing-up days. Sometimes we would visit his nearby relatives and the cemetery where my grandmother's parents are buried. Then we'd walk to his town house for Sunday night church, 7UP® floats, and "The Ed Sullivan Show." I would spend the night in their big guest room bed and then walk to school the next day.

My grandfather is a symbol of unconditional love, always there for me, supporting and loving me in good times and bad. I did not spend much time with him after I left my hometown and went away to college and medical school. He, however, never forgot me and sent me letters every week on his 30-year-old typewriter with intermittent keys that barely print. Every other sentence ended with etc, etc, etc. Each letter was filled with stories of his experiences away from home in

World War I and words of love and encouragement. Always enclosed was a dollar bill. When he suffered this stroke twenty years later, I am devastated. I cannot bear to lose the love which I knew he showed to me no matter what I had done.

I walk into my grandfather's hospital room for the first time. There is an immediate look of astonishment on his face. I believe he knows me even though he never again shows any sign of recognition. As I sit by his bed and listen to his labored breathing, I feel helpless. What can I do? All my years of medical practice do not give me answers. I remember his faith tradition and honor it by reading the Psalms aloud, beginning with this first Psalm. I am embarrassed when personnel come into the room, but an inner voice says this is what my grandfather wants to hear. I am calmed. This is what I would want at my deathbed-- to hear the Psalms read by someone who loves me.

My grandfather's illness and death become a major turning point in my life. This is the beginning of my journey in earnest seeking to find a connection with a power greater than myself. I desperately want to believe that somehow I will stay connected to my grandfather, and my tradition tells me this might be possible through a belief in a God. I cannot bear the thought of never again knowing the love I received from my grandfather. I want to return to my tradition and begin a new spiritual journey. My grandfather's unconditional love leads me back to the unconditional love of a God. We now begin this journey reading the Psalms together. We will be "trees planted together by streams of water," hoping to bear fruit in our season.

What do these Psalms mean to you? For me they are readings that I can turn to when I need to give or receive comfort. When I read this first Psalm, I return to my grandfather's hospital room reading this passage to him. I feel his love, even in his unconscious state, as I read to him words he loved and shared with me in his daily living.

Remember today someone who first showed you a glimpse of the unconditional love that you long to receive from your God. If they are alive, call or write and thank them. If they are dead, give thanks for them.

Psalm 2
"Why do the nations conspire, and the peoples plot in vain?"

My husband and I begin our careers at a newly formed Children's Hospital. Within a few weeks of arrival, I am determined that our hospital have a specific pediatric physician on staff. I know without a doubt that this growing hospital will not be a medical center of excellence without the immediate presence of this type of specialty doctor. Difficulty after difficulty keeps us from bringing this specialty of physician to our state, but I persist, and finally she comes. I and everyone else soon realize it is a disaster. She is not the right person. The timing is not right. The support team is not there.

Several years later. One of our children does not want to return to college. My husband and I do everything possible, spend large amounts of money, and send her to Europe in hopes that she will change her mind, and finally tell her we can not support her if she does not return to college. Our manipulation does not work, and at last we surrender and give up. Five years later, she returns to college with a desire for learning that is beyond any concept we could have given her. She graduates with honors and now has finished a graduate degree.

Persistence is one of my major virtues, but I am beginning to see it sometimes is also a liability. For years I have tried to push forth my programs, my ideas at my work and in my family. I have recently realized that when stumbling block after stumbling block is put in my path, I should pay attention and back off. The time may not be right. The plan may be off. Taking action is hard work, but doors seem to open when plans are right.

I am gradually learning that I know very little of our God's plan for my life and know even less of God's plan for others, even those whom I deeply love. When a plan is not a plot, doors open, serendipity happens, and there are moments of affirmation along the way, even when the course is lined with rocks and crevices. Pathways that seem beyond reach become possible.

Ponder doors in your life that have shut. Should you wait for a possible new door to open before crashing through the old door?

Psalm 3

"But thou, O LORD, art a shield about me,
and my glory, and the lifter of my head.
I cry aloud to the LORD,
and he answers me from his holy hill."

We are on a holiday weekend at a country retreat house. I wake up at this mountaintop respite, sit on the deck with my cup of coffee, and watch the white cloudy mist rise and gradually uncover the green valley below. The quiet and the stillness are as moving as a Brahms symphony. I am wearing old, loose clothes. I am peaceful and comfortable. My spiritual friend often tells me to wear life like a loose garment. I understand now what she means. I feel life hanging next to me like my loose dress. My spiritual friend tries to tell me not to take life so seriously, to lighten up, that I may not be as big a deal as I think. For so long, life has been a tight garment where every move I make is of utmost importance, affecting my life and the lives of others. I think back on my week. I think of problems that consumed me for days. Most have reached some solution or are stable, and I am now consumed by new difficulties that are agonizing me like the original ones. If only I could trust that answers will come and that I don't need to be in such a state of constant anxiety. My agonizing also did not bring on the solutions. I hope I can remember the metaphor of the loose garment when I return to the city and the real world. I seem to need so many physical and mental images to remind me what this life is all about. These are guideposts to lead me in my blindness, to keep me on the path that God has chosen for me.

Today wear loose clothes and lighten up. Consider that you and your decisions may not be as important as you think you are.

Psalm 4
"How long will you love vain words and seek after lies?"

She is in her late seventies. As you walk into her cottage you immediately see the glow coming from her bleached hair destroyed by the southern summer sun and years of chemical dyes. Her face is deeply wrinkled and sags like worn out leather, destroyed by years of smoking. She is dressed is the usual multicolor, gaudy, flashy, tasteless outfit. Her huge body fills the chair and the room with a suffocating tightness that makes it difficult for others to breathe or talk.

Maybe I am afraid or cannot talk.

Experience tells me she will cry uncontrollably, throw things, yell, scream, and have a tantrum like a child if you do not do what she wants you to do. Some say she has never grown up. In fact, her house is like a doll house, stuffed with bazaar art craft, plastic flowers, garage sale treasures, and every possible doll made in the last century. She is incapable of being honest. She is not in touch with reality and her surroundings. She takes one of the first trips into China when it opens to tourists, and all she talks about on her return is how much her feet hurt.

At this visit like all the others, she constantly wants to be waited on. One of her friends is also visiting. Strange how with each visit, there is a different friend. None seem to stay for any length of time. Her idea of truth is whatever will make her look her best. Her life is totally centered on herself.

When I call her on the phone, each time, I think it will be different. She will want to know about my family and what we are doing. Instead she only wants to talk about what is going on in her life. I think back to failed attempts to let her know my true feelings met by the pity reserved for a wounded animal. I remember her pouting lip, the tears, the pitiful, "you don't love me" look and the "after all I have done for you"

11

words. Her development seems to be arrested at an early childhood level. Recently she has had several life-threatening illnesses where she is given a chance to change her life. Nothing changes. She cannot accept responsibility for her own life.

I learn from this one person so much, namely what can happen when honesty is absent and self is at the center of our life. My image of her is like a little bird on my shoulder reminding me when I am tempted to stretch or change the truth: "This is what happens when you become incapable of being honest." She is a reminder of what I do not want to be. After many years I finally see her as a wounded person, like a wounded, helpless bird that for many reasons could not leave the nest. Sometimes, however, I am horrified to see myself in her image. I catch myself doing some of the same unkind and selfish acts. I look in the mirror and see myself wearing a bizarre outfit. I have started dyeing my hair. I tell small lies to put myself in the right light. I fail to ask others what is happening in their lives and instead only talk about myself. I become upset when my family doesn't do what I want them to do.

My prayer today is that honesty will become a part of my being. I pray that I will be able to admit my mistakes and shortcomings. I pray that I will be less self centered. I also pray that I will be aware and not blind to the many second chances God gives me to make changes in my own life to overcome these shortcomings before I harm others and myself. I also pray to see goodness, love, and the ever present light of God in this person that is there but so hidden from my sight by the years of darkness.

Pray for honesty for yourself to see and accept the reality of life. Pray that you will be aware of God's daily second chances and wake up calls to change.

Psalm 5

"Lead me, O LORD, in your righteousness...
Let all who take refuge in you rejoice;
let them ever sing for joy.
Spread your protection over them."

Experience tells you if you decide to go outside to the beach and to the sea, you must first put on some kind of protection from the heat of the day or you will get burned. The surf does not look too high from your safe haven, your house near the beach, but when you actually go down to the shoreline, the waves are as tall as buildings or even mountains. Some who are with you decide not to venture into the surf. It is too awesome, too dangerous. They sit down in the sand on shore. Some build sand castles. Others never leave the safety of their home and decide not to go to the beach at all. But you want to make the plunge. You have been given a moment of clarity that calls you to step into the blue-green sea that looks endless and unknown. The surf is foamy and furiously close to the shore as you first enter. There is less space between the pounding waves. You learn from the adventuresome that the best way to make it through the cascading waves is to move with the waves, dive into them, ride them, and then swim out a little farther before the next one comes. If you just stand there, the powerful wave will usually knock you down. There is no way around this movable wall. Sometimes a jellyfish stings you. The sting is at times so painful that you must go back to shore, rest in the sand, and apply some tenderizer before going back out. You try again. You learn it is safer and it also helps to go out with a buddy who can support you. Finally you are now just a little beyond the breaking waves. You lie on your back and surrender your body to the saltwater. You surrender to something unbelievably greater than yourself. You float with the current and the tide and experience a peace beyond understanding, letting go and allowing the ocean to carry you into the next wave. And then you start all over again. Sooner than you think, it is your turn to take out a new friend, a child, a grandchild with you to teach them the technique of riding the waves. Sooner than you think your body is too worn out to venture into the sea. You find inner peace now by just surrendering to the shore and watching and cheering on old and new buddies, encouraging them not to be afraid to venture into the ever-changing sea. The ride, the surrender is all worth it. No regrets.

Pray this prayer three times today:
God, I offer myself to Thee-
To build with me and to do with me as Thou wilt.
Relieve me of the bondage of self,
that I may better do Thy will.
Take away my difficulties,
That victory over them may bear witness to those I would help of Thy Power,
Thy Love, and Thy Way of life.
May I do Thy will always![1]

Psalm 6

"O LORD, do not rebuke me in your anger,
or discipline me in your wrath.
Be gracious to me, O LORD, for I am languishing:
O LORD, heal me, for my bones are shaking with terror."

A spiritual friend, Jane Wolfe, tells me that if I am hurt in a car accident, the person who has harmed me is usually not the same person who brings me healing. If I am seriously hurt, I will go to a hospital and get professional help. My physical recovery from an accident may also take some time with the help of friends and family and many others. I learn in 12-step programs that this is also true of recovery from my addictions, my resentments, my character defects, and my broken relationships. If I do not forgive someone who has harmed me, they are still harming me in the resentment I carry like a heavy backpack. I must forgive the one who has harmed me, but I cannot expect that person also to be the one to heal me. That will come later from another person, if I will accept it. My fantasy, however, is that the person who harmed me will also heal me. He or she is usually incapable of this, but I seem to keep wanting them to, especially if they are family members or close friends. Our relationship remains strained while I wait for the healing from them that will never come. I also must accept the reverse situation. I may not be able to heal those whom I have harmed. I must make amends for hurt I have brought to friends, my family, my husband, my children, my partners, but I probably will not be the one who brings them healing. What I can do is make living amends, letting them know I am a different person by the new life I am living.

Pray that you can forgive those who have injured you. Ask for forgiveness and make amends to those you have harmed. Look

15

for and be open to healing for yourself and for others from other people.

Psalm 7

"O LORD my God, if I have done this,
if there is wrong in my hands,
if I have repaid my ally with harm or plundered my foe
without cause,
then let the enemy pursue and overtake me."

At least twice a week she comes to my reading station to point out an error I have made reading an X-ray. Some days I graciously accept that I made a mistake. At other times I am devastated by my imperfection. Her critical and judgmental behavior does not change. It is my inner critic that changes. It is my reaction to what she says that is different from day to day.

I strive for perfection. Imperfection is my enemy. I have tried many medications to relieve the pain that comes when I make a mistake in my life. Working at the hospital until late into the night to prove I am a good physician, returning home to work into the wee hours, smoking two packs of cigarettes a day, double chocolate ice cream and peanuts, fine and not so fine white wines, shopping for distinctive one-of-a-kind dresses, scarves, and earrings are only a few of my favorite medications of choice as I deal with my imperfection. They are only temporary solutions and often produce more pain eventually than the original difficulty. Often the pain I feel is for some wrong I have done to myself or to another with very good intentions. Making amends gives me greater relief than all these other medications I have tried, and it usually brings relief sooner.

My spiritual friend teaches me that admitting to another person that I have done something wrong allows me to take off that mask of perfection where I try to pretend to be something I am not. "I made a mistake in my diagnosis of what is going on with your patient. I hope I have learned from this and will do better next time." Admitting my mistakes allows me to feel my humanity. I learn I am not God. There is no halo above my head. I will make mistakes. Being aware of my own humanness also keeps me sensitive to the humanity in others and sometimes even keeps me from being so judgmental.

I am gradually learning to trust painful times, conflicts with others, as signs to address issues. "I have lost my job. What was my part in this? What can I learn? Is there some other work or another company that I am better suited for? Do I need to make amends to those I formerly worked with before I move on?" I usually find the answer with prayer and by talking to a spiritual friend. This inner pain that has been my enemy has become an outward stop or HALT sign for me that I am not on the right path and may need to stop and make amends.

Is there someone with whom you should make amends? Ask God to lead you to the answer.

Psalm 8

"When I look at your heavens,
the work of your fingers,
the moon and the stars that you have established;
what are human beings that you are mindful of them,
mortals that you care for them?
Yet you have made them a little lower than God,
and crowned them with glory and honor."

I walk outside into the early morning, look up and out to the blue cloudless sky, hear the early morning bird's wake up call, smell the honeysuckle and magnolias, and walk through a path of trees reaching almost to the sky. The music, the smells, the pointing overlapping trees remind me that I am in nature's ancient cathedral. After a few minutes I realize that this adventure outside is more healing for my soul and body than any known drug or substance. When I walk or sit outside and observe the world, the sunrise, the sunset, or the foamy sea, my mood becomes more uplifted, my depression ceases. When I cannot sleep because of some inner or outer situation, my mind is quieted and calmed by sitting by my window or on my porch and watching the sun slowly rise and the darkness is changed from black to gray to pink to red to orange and then bright light. I am reminded that daylight will always come even out of the darkest moment. This is God's daily promise to us. When I am outside, I am aware that there is something greater than the problems that consume and threaten my life. There is a higher plan. The warmth of the sun, the cooing of the birds, the smell of fresh cedar, or the constant roar of the waves reminds me of a mystery greater than I can imagine. What is consuming me and blocking me from God loses some of its power. I am aware of a world, a power, greater than my obsessions and myself. For that brief period of time when I am aware of the world outside of me, my world does not revolve around my problems and my self.

This is a healing gift from God always available if we only choose to accept it. My greatest nightmare is being confined to a prison with no windows to the outside. Some days I can best appreciate and cry out for the heavens when I become aware that I have confined myself that day to a situation that has become like a prison, literally or figuratively. Relief is immediately available outside.

Today take a walk or sit or look outside and be aware of the power greater than yourself who created this earth.

Psalm 9

"You are the one who lifts me up from the gates of death, so that I may recount all your praises."

I mourn the death of a relationship. I have a friend who was once almost part of my being. We were closer than family. We now rarely see each other. He has become so busy in his work there is no time for our relationship. I am angry because I miss him and his love. I am jealous of the things, the business, and the work that has separated us. I long for the closeness we once had. I talk to another spiritual friend about it. Today as I walk in the cool of the morning by the ever-changing seashore, I think about her words to me the night before. What is my part in the loss of this relationship? I was too busy to be with this friend at times as well. There are amends I need to make to him. I wonder how many other relationships I have also missed because I was too busy, too important to nurture them. I ponder my part in this lost relationship. Instead of obsessing about the loss of this relationship, I plan to make amends for my part in this loss, and I rejoice in the time we had together. I know that few people have had such a wonderful friend as I had. I also feel great gratitude for the part my friend had in bringing me back to a relationship with God. I think of friends I have known who have lost family members, especially children. Their grief is overwhelming. They seem to find a resurrection place, however, when their thoughts change from a concentration on what they have lost to a gratitude for the time, the experience they had together, even so briefly.

Give thanks today for past relationships with people who showed you unconditional love and taught you about God. Give thanks for the relationships new and old you have found in your life.

21

Psalm 10

"Their eyes stealthily watch for the helpless;
they lurk in secret like a lion in its covert;
they lurk that they may seize the poor;
they seize the poor and drag them off in their net."

I look out from a balcony overlooking the Alabama Gulf Coast and observe the world outside of myself. The constant rhythm of the waves slows my frantically racing life and heartbeat. The brown pelicans swoop by in their distinctive parade patterns in pairs or in groups. They fly so close to the ocean that their wingtips must sometimes get wet. They flap their large wings for several strokes and then glide. That is what this time at the beach is, a time to glide after weeks and months of flapping. I am fascinated by the laughing gulls that stick by the pelicans, as if they were best friends. They follow the brown pelicans in their spectacular plunging dive for their dinner. Then the gulls shamelessly and expertly try to snatch the fish directly out of the pelican's enormous bill before he can swallow it. Ouch! This is too reminiscent of the life I am escaping from. Am I a laughing gull or brown pelican? Some days a gull, some days a pelican.

Another flock of brown pelicans fly right by my window on their way home for the night. Their silent majestic flight leaves me speechless as well. The adults do not have a voice. Only their young nestlings speak with loud grunts and screams.

Tonight take inventory for the day, pray for awareness of times when as an adult you have failed to speak out for a truth you screamed out for as a youth. Pray for awareness of times you have taken credit for something that someone else has accomplished.

Psalm 11
"In the LORD I take refuge;
...For the Lord is righteous;
he loves righteous deeds;
the upright shall behold his face."

I sit in the doctor's office procedure room waiting for surgery my primary physician has recommended. Everything is foreign. I do not know the people in this office, and they do not know me. I am not at home as in my own physician's office. They call me by my first name. Most other places I am recognized by my titles, Mrs., Dr., Rev. I have lost my identity. I am no longer special. I have only a vague idea of what they will be doing. I only know it is something I need to have done. I feel alone and frightened. A fearful memory from the past returns. I am a little girl alone in a hospital room, crying. It was standard procedure when I was a child that parents did not stay with their children. I look out into the wooded area beyond the treatment room and say my prayers. The answer that comes is "surrender." This is what surrender is all about. Giving into something that you are told will be best for you and stepping out into an unknown that many others have done and had good results. I close my eyes. The doctor and the nurse come in; the procedure begins. I begin to trust that "all will be well, all will be well, and all will be well."

Remember a time when you were seeking refuge. Remember times of surrender you have had and the difference it made.

Psalm 12

**"May the LORD cut off all flattering lips,
the tongue that makes great boasts,
those who say, 'With our tongues we will prevail;
our lips are our own—who is our master?' "**

Our state's weekly business newspaper put out a list each year of the 100 top women in the state. I am on their list for several years. Then one year I am not. This bothers me. I become aware how much I need recognition, affirmation from others. I talk to a friend. She confides similar feelings. We laugh together over our insatiable craving for approval and recognition and share the times we have felt rejected. We joke about our star shaped earrings we will wear at our next social event to make light of our shortcomings. Today we have been made aware of some of our defects and have prayed to be changed. In the meantime, God may be using us even in the midst of our defects. My desperate need for recognition in my work may have helped to heal some of the children I see. My need to perform the harp may have brought peace to some. God wastes nothing. I also know that I have found nothing that will completely fill that hole inside of me for recognition—no award, no event, no appearances, no writings bring lasting peace. The only "filler" for that hole is an awareness of God's unconditional love. I only have peace when I am aware that God loves me just as I am, not for who or what I am or what I do. I know this in my head. I wait for God to reveal it to my heart. In the meantime, I hope to stay aware of these shortcomings and pray that God will change me.

Pray for the peace that comes with knowing God's unconditional love for you.

Psalm 13

"How long must I bear pain in my soul,
and have sorrow in my heart all day long?
How long shall my enemy be exalted over me?
Consider and answer me, O LORD, my God!
Give light to my eyes."

I met with an old friend I have become reacquainted with. She openly shares with me some of her story. We now are separated by very different educational levels, lifestyles, professions, and spirituality. Our life difficulties are similar, however: illness, difficult family members, intimacy in relationships, resentments. I learn much from her experience. She teaches me about boundaries. She does not dwell on self-pity or the difficulties of her situation. She tells me she has learned from the difficult people she must work with on a daily basis. She is determined to make her life meaningful and complete, be alert to changes she must make, work out solutions, and seek help for herself and her family. The difficult people she deals with have become icons, guideposts, and reminders of what she does not want to be. She does not see their lives as wasted, for their inability to change has made her change. She deals with difficult people as best she can, tries not to pass judgment, and strives to make her own life different. I am slowly learning that God sends answers to prayers where I least expect it. I wonder how many times I missed God's answer because I was looking for it in an educated person from my own background. Tonight in my prayers I pray that God will heal me of my prejudices.

Spend some time today truly listening to someone at work or an old friend whom you have neglected because you do not share a similar lifestyle or professions or economic background.

Psalm 14

"The fool says in his heart, 'There is no God,'...
The LORD looks down from heaven upon the children of men,
to see if there are any that act wisely,
that seek after God."

Carl Jung had carved in Latin over the front door of his home in Zurich, *Bidden or not bidden, God is present.* The words were also carved on Jung's tombstone. My husband gave me a plaque of the carving, which we have placed in the living room of a mountain retreat overlooking a spectacular view of the Arkansas River Valley. It is hard not to hear and see God at this holy place. Much of my writing has been done on this mountaintop. Jung's words remind us that the God we touch on this sacred mountain will be with us as we descend to the valley, even when we do not honor him or acknowledge him or call for him. We do not lose that love. It is always there. It is also with our friends and family as they depart from us.

Give thanks for the unbelievable love God constantly gives us.

Psalm 15

"O LORD, who may abide in your tent?
...Those who speak the truth from their heart;
who do not slander with their tongue,
and do no evil to their friends."

I meet with a small group where we share our experience, strength, and hope about our attempts at connection with God. I arrive burdened by the cares of the day and leave filled with peace and strength to live that day with the best tools given me. Why am I so healed by this experience? For that one hour, the committee in my head becomes less demanding and chatty. It turns its head to listen to another committee outside of me where my mind and heart have previously heard words of strength and hope. I have learned that God calls me to community. When I am deaf to God's voice inside of me, that power speaks more clearly through the voice of someone else. When I am blind to God's vision, God shines even more brightly through the example and experience of another. When I am burdened by life's trials, I hear others speak and realize I am not alone with this problem, and always there are others with much more difficult trials than mine.

Give thanks for your group where you share your journey. If you don't yet have a group, ask God to show you one.

Psalm 16
**"I bless the LORD, who gives me counsel;
in the night also my heart instructs me."**

Every tradition is filled with stories of how God speaks to people in their dreams. It is one of many ways that God reaches out to us. Dreams are an important part of the spiritual life of some and have less meaning for others, just as some find connection with God through yoga or centering prayer or a rosary or walking or fasting, while others find these disciplines difficult. How wonderful that our God has chosen so many ways to communicate with us!

Dreams are sometimes the most difficult for me to work with, for they are time consuming. I want instant answers and dream work is "work," often with another friend or group. Today I am remembering one of my favorite dreams: My daughter is a young girl and is HIV+. I am taking blood from her for a test and the needle sticks me. I panic. An older, experienced nurse from a VA hospital comes in and tells me exactly what to do. She gives me a blue solution that is an antidote to the illness.

As I work through this dream for many weeks with a friend, we realize the blue antidote to a fatal illness for the child within me (represented by my daughter) is the sky and blue water, the outdoors, the ocean, nature. This has proven true for me. The more time I spend outside being nurtured by God's natural beauty, the more peace I feel, the more love and gratitude I know. Outdoors under the immense blue sky and forest canopy, I become aware of a power greater than myself. Inside at my desk, my world often re-centers on me. What a beautiful, life-changing, life-saving message from God that came in "the music of the night."

Write down your dream from last night. Mediate during the day on what your higher power may be revealing to you in this night message from the heart.

Psalm 17

"Guard me as the apple of the eye;
hide me in the shadow of your wings.
... I shall behold your face in righteousness;
when I awake I shall be satisfied, beholding your likeness."

The first two lines of Psalm 17 are part of night time prayers called Compline read at the end of the day. As I recite the Psalm, I remember friends we have read Compline with as we end the day together. I feel protected and safe when I hear these verses, "the apple (seen in the pupil) of God's eye, hidden under the shadow of God's wings." God sees us and is there to guide and protect and care for us, if only we will allow it. What continues to baffle me is how I still try to rely on myself rather than God. I do not believe the work will get done unless I do it. I often must force myself to take time for daily prayer and meditation at the start of each morning. I am so busy. I must get started on the day's work before I take time off to pray. I know in my heart that my strength for the day begins with this meditation time. I have no hope of accomplishing my tasks without connecting to this strength from God, but yet I fight it.

Today I am on vacation at the beach. Even here I think of so many little jobs I need to do before I take time to be quiet with God. My salvation is that at least God has given me awareness of this struggle. My daily prayer is that I will be changed and realize the source of any strength I may possess to perform the tasks my Creator has planned for me.

Pray for an awareness of God's plan for your life and pray for the strength to carry it out.

Psalm 18

"He reached down from on high, he took me; ...
He brought me into a broad place;
he delivered me, because he delighted in me."

My husband and I are on vacation away from work. I am reading a non-medical book, Margaret Truman's *First Ladies*. I read about one of the first ladies who was active in the Women's Missionary Society. I remember immediately my grandmother and her missionary society meetings and how much I loved going with her. I have no idea why I enjoyed going, except that I received so much unconditional love whenever I was around my grandparents. Their eyes brightened when I came to their door. They stopped whatever they were doing, welcomed me, and just wanted to talk about what was going on in my world.

I cannot remember anything about the substance of my grandmother's meetings. I remember only the warmth of her friends, her four sisters and the older women five times my age who invited me into their Victorian homes with dark velvet drapes and marble tables. I was offered cake, cookies, ice cream, spice tea and love served on intricately painted white china dishes on a lace tablecloth. I still feel enveloped, encircled by the warmth and love of those meetings.

We also visit New Orleans. As I look at the weather-worn wood of the older houses in the Garden District, I remember the historic colonial farmhouse on my grandparents' farm. Mostly I remember the comfort of the love from the people who lived there. My grandparents are still "reaching down from on high" and loving me long after their deaths. I also feel God loved me, delighted in me so often through my grandparents. I still feel the delight of God through those dear people.

Give thanks today for those whom God has chosen to love and delight in you. Give thanks for God's love manifested so beautifully through the love of others. Pray that you will also be able to give that love — long after your death.

Psalm 19
"But who can detect their errors?
Clear me from hidden faults."

I remember the first time my husband and I have the inside of our vacation house painted. Actually, our rental agency suggests it. The once-pristine white walls have not been painted for ten years since we first bought the condominium on the Gulf coast. It is rented much of the time, but our family escapes to this beach paradise several weeks during the year. Each trip we talk about painting the gradually deteriorating walls but always put it off. Each time we arrive, we think we must do the painting this time, but by the end of the visit, the surroundings don't appear so worn. Next time. Finally our manger gives us the number for the painter, and we call him. He walks into the condo and immediately comments on the spectacular view of the ocean and the beach from our windows and balcony. However, as he goes through the apartment to give us the estimate, he begins to point out areas of much needed repair we have never noticed. We can't believe it. We suddenly see walls we have looked at for years, never noticing the many black furniture scars, red crayon marks, and dents where doors and furniture hit the white walls. This is especially evident in several of our closets where suitcases and beach equipment were weekly put in and removed.

I talk to a spiritual friend about the awareness. She shares how this may also ring true in our lives. First we have some awareness of a character defect. We think about changing it, but often it becomes such a familiar part of us that we more and more overlook the defect. It blends in with the rest of our being. It becomes comfortable. We never realize most of our character defects, as if they are hidden in some closet. This is where a spiritual advisor, a good friend, a counselor, a 12-step sponsor can be so important. We need some friend who, like our vacation house painter, can gently show us these faults, faults that are so obvious to others but so hidden from us. Often these spiritual friends only need to reflect to us our behavior, and the character defect is obvious. Sometimes they may guide us to a realization to the defect in ourselves in our over-reaction to the character defects of another person. Sometimes they will directly confront us. Sometimes we must even call in a professional to point us back on the road when our humanness has become unmarketable.

Spiritual friends, like our painter, reassure and support us by pointing out our beauty marks as well when they are not obvious to us.

Give thanks for and seek out spiritual friends who can speak to you with honesty.

Psalm 20
"May he grant you your desire and fulfill all your plans."

This is a perfect day and a perfect Psalm to read to celebrate an achievement. I see families reading this Psalm at the birth of a child. I see politicians reading this Psalm after winning an election. I see Olympic athletes reading the Psalm with close friends after a great victory. What a Psalm of hope for years to come after a great triumph.

This also is a Psalm about every day for everyone in recovery. Each day that we do not drink or use drugs or are involved in whatever addiction has taken over our lives is a day to celebrate and be grateful. "One day at a time."

Too often when I have achieved a goal, I do not stop to celebrate and give praise and gratitude for the accomplishment. I am too busy getting ready for the next goal, the next day. But God wants us to celebrate! There is a time to celebrate victory, and there is a time to admit our shortcomings. The loneliness of Psalm 22 is on the next page, but today is the day to celebrate. This is also a wonderful Psalm to remind us of God's part in our accomplishment and to be grateful.

Read this Psalm today when you reach a goal, and celebrate.

Psalm 21

**"You have given him his heart's desire,
and have not withheld the request of his lips."**

Heart? I am a physician. I know what the physical heart looks like. I know its appearance when there is pathology, and I have personal experience with its diseased state. I have a family history of heart disease. My mother died in heart failure. I try to watch my diet and exercise to prevent this potential problem in me.

What is the symbolic heart? Is it a feeling, is it an emotion? Is it love? Is the heart the symbol for the love which the apostle Paul describes as something which "never ends, which bears all things, believes all things, hopes all things, endures all things?"

The Tin Man went on his journey with Dorothy in search of a heart in the Wizard of Oz. Eastern Orthodox tradition tells us "Let your mind descend into the heart." St. Benedict tells us to listen to God with "the ear of our heart." The presider at Christian communion services often says, "Lift up your hearts."

Hebrew and Christian Testament writings ask us not to "harden your heart." The Psalmist tells us that he "hates those with a divided heart." The book of Joel tells us to "rend your hearts and not your garments." The book of Samuel tells us that "the Lord does not see as mortals see; they look on the outward appearance, but the Lord looks on the heart." In Jeremiah, God tells us "I will put my law within them, and I will write it on their hearts, and I will be their God, and they shall be my people." In Psalm 51 the writer prays that God "will create in me a clean heart." After the visit of the shepherds, Mary "pondered these things in her heart" at our Lord's birth. The Song of Solomon asks that you "set me as a seal upon your heart." Jesus tells us in the Beatitudes, "Blessed are the pure in heart, for they shall see God." In Psalm 16 we are told "in the night also my heart instructs me."

Is the heart symbolic for something that is the counterpart of head knowledge? Is it Spirit? Is it intuition? Is it wholeness? It is a mystery. I only know it is something I desire. I am the Tin Man on a journey looking for my heart and the heart of God. I sometimes find it in myself. I more often feel it and see it in others. I see into the hearts of so many other role models. Then I "fake it" and act as if I have a heart. Then it sometimes comes.

C. S. Lewis tells us to "act as if." Most of the time I feel as if I have an artificial heart. My prayer is that the real one will be transplanted into me someday.

Pray that you may see the heart of God in yourself and in your neighbor today.

Psalm 22

"For he did not despise or abhor the afflictions of the
afflicted;
he did not hide his face from me,
but heard when I cried to him."

I hurry up the steps of the National Gallery of Art. I
have only a few minutes before the gallery closes. Before I
leave Washington I must visit an old friend, my favorite
painting. I turn to the right, past the Flemish, past early
Christian art. Alas, it is still there in a room with early French
artists! It is Georges de La Tour's "The Repentant
Magdalene.²" Mary Magdalene sits in a darkened room
wearing a loose-fitting, cream-colored blouse. She leans into a
table touching a human skull with one hand and peers into a
mirror. Her left hand is touching the face of the skull elevated
on a closed book. Magdalene's chin rests on her right hand.
The dried skull almost completely hides the only light in the
room, a low burning candle. The reflection of the skull is seen
in the mirror. Magdalene stares meditatively into the mirror in
front of her. I have talked so often to friends about this
painting. What is the skull? Does the dried human skull
represent our dried-up humanity, our character defects?
Magdalene can feel the dead skull, her inhumanity, with her
body, her hand, but she can not look directly at it. She only
sees the dead face in reflection, in a mirror. There she studies
the dry bones skull. She is not disgusted by it, simply studies
it, is aware of it. Each visit I identify with Magdalene and want
to learn more from her. I can feel my inhuman nature and my
dry bones dead defects as Magdalene does, but often I cannot
see it. I am only aware of my inhumanness as it is reflected in
others. I often cannot see my own character defects in myself,
but I become aware of them when I see them reflected in
others, selfishness, need to control, self-centeredness. When I

over-react or am especially overwhelmed by a fault in another, I have learned that the reflection of that defect may very well also be in me. This is one of the mysteries of how God works in our lives, often putting us in contact with people who have similar defects that we often fail to see in ourselves. We are given the opportunity "to see through a glass darkly."

In your meditative time today, ponder some character defect you abhor in another. Is it also one of your own defects you have not yet acknowledged?

Psalm 23
"The LORD is my shepherd, I shall not want."

I return to the National Cathedral and immediately go to my favorite chapel. It is the Chapel of the Good Shepherd. It once was open twenty-four hours a day. It is still the most accessible worship space, open until ten at night. It is a very small chapel with a stone-carved statue over the altar of the good shepherd gently holding a lamb in his arms. The lamb is resting, not fighting the tender touch supporting him. There are only pews for about six people in the chapel. Pilgrims often have left evidences of their visits. Sometimes I have found wildflowers on the altar, sometimes handwritten notes, and once there was a small nutcracker soldier at Christmas time.

Shepherds and lambs are not the significant part of our culture that they were in Christ's day. We relate very loosely to these images, but I do connect to this particular statue. The face and hands of the good shepherd have been stained and worn by human oil from the touch of so many hands of pilgrims to this worship place. The shepherd's hands and face have taken on a human appearance. It is a powerful sight. It is a holy place. We virtually see the cries and tears of so many who have transformed the face and hands of the shepherd. The statue speaks to me. I am not the only needy person in the world. I feel a bond with the petitions of all who have entered that chapel and reached out to the Good Shepherd for healing. I feel connected through my humanness, the oil of our bodies, to so many others who also are desperately seeking a shepherd for this journey.

Find an image of God as the Good Shepherd and contemplate what it may mean in your life.

Psalm 24

"The earth is the LORD's and all that is in it,
the world, and those who live in it;
for he has founded it on the seas,
and established it on the rivers."

I am at a retreat at a conference center in the quiet mountains of North Carolina. I must leave early to go to a business meeting in Chicago. The second day it begins to snow. I obsess about whether I will be able to get to my business meeting and spend the day worrying about whether I will be able to get out of this beautiful place. I am obsessing about the weather, something over which I have absolutely no control. The conference is on meditative techniques of Eastern religions. I am in desperate need this day for these practices. I sit and walk in silence. As smoke rises from the incense at the altar, these obsessions rise within me. My mantra is to be relieved of this obsession, to be able to live and enjoy the beautiful present. A spiritual advisor tells me to see my obsessions as barges going down a river. I am told not to try to banish them, but to stop and gather them in and ask them as they appear, "Hello; what can I learn from you?" These obsessions teach me that control is still a huge factor in my life. I acknowledge this and try to go on.

Consider sitting or walking in silence for a brief period today. As thoughts pass through your mind, honor them and ask them what you can learn from these interruptions. Let them rise like incense or smoke and move on like barges down the Mississippi or the river closest to you.

Psalm 25

"Do not let me be put to shame;
... For your name's sake, O LORD,
pardon my guilt, for it is great.
... Relieve the troubles of my heart."

I was heavily involved in my addiction to work and alcohol when my children were in their growing up years. I worked ten hours a day, came home and had two glasses of wine before dinner, two during dinner, two after dinner, then went to sleep, and with few exceptions started the whole process over again early the next day. At the few intervals when I had some awareness of what I was doing, shame became an integral part of the cycle. One of my children would get into trouble or act out, and I realized I had no relationship with them. Those overwhelming feelings of "I am a bad person" would come over me like a tidal wave or tsunami and consume me. I had the sensation that I was drowning in my addiction. It is comforting that the Psalmist so many years ago fought this battle. The Psalmist also gives us the same answer that is part of the 12-steps of recovery. We seek a relationship with God, we ask for forgiveness for the wrongs we have done, and we seek relief by leading a new life with a new heart.

Shame is also part of our external culture. I daily work with people who feel good about themselves by shaming or pointing out others' mistakes. I learn that I must wear a little tougher skin when I am around these people. As I get to know them better I realize that they have been very wounded, shamefully. They have been exposed to someone who relished in pointing out *their* mistakes. Shaming *others* has become their defense. I see what can happen if this shame pattern is not broken.

I do not believe the God I know desires that I feel shame about my life or myself. I am given the option to ask for "pardon for my guilt" instead of drowning in my mistakes, and the troubles of my heart can be relieved. I am not God. I am human. I will make mistakes. If I can admit to them, ask for forgiveness, and not pretend that I am perfection, I have a chance at peace. This is what some describe as "the spirituality of imperfection."

Confess your character defects to yourself, God, and another person; ask for forgiveness to those you have harmed if to do so will not bring them more harm. Do not allow others to fill your cup with shame.

Psalm 26

"Prove me, O LORD, and try me;
Test my heart and mind.
For your steadfast love is before my eyes,
and I walk in faithfulness to you."

I compulsively begin working this week on a project that is due in several months. Once I start working on the project, I cannot stop. I avoid my regular work assignments; I miss or am late for meetings, one with my spiritual friend. She tells me this may be what 12-step groups call "self-will run riot." I become so focused on my issues I can not think of anything else but my will, my plan. It is a character defect. As with all truths in life, it has a positive and a negative. Being able to be focused is a great attribute and can allow me to accomplish many things. The negative shift occurs when focus is so narrow that there is no room for anybody or anything else. I become incapable of being open to anything God might present to me in the present moment that is not part of my plan. I become so obsessed with this one issue I have difficulty performing my required daily routine or interacting with others I work with or meet during my day.

The solution is making a change in my life by turning my life and my will over to God. What is God's will? How do I distinguish it from my will? I still remember the haunting words of a seasoned spiritual director, "Beware of anyone who tells you he know God's will." It is too great a knowledge for one person to know. I have learned not to depend on myself, but to talk to others and to discern questions in my community, in particular with a spiritual friend. My experience is that I only have a glimpse of God's will after a situation has occurred and I reflect upon it. While I am in the problem or solution I do not know with certainty that this is God's will. I have a vague sense of peace that keeps guiding me. I am not as anxious. I have a comfortable feeling in my body that this is right, but I still feel as if I am "looking through a glass darkly." I also know that when I am "absolutely certain" that this is what God wants me to do, I am usually mistaken.

Pray for knowledge of when you are living in self will. Ask a spiritual friend to help you with this.

Psalm 27
**"Teach me you way, O LORD,
and lead me on a level path because of my enemies."**

I no longer must go to a traditional classroom to be taught. Instead I share a meal with several friends and we eventually talk about how we are all finding a connection to God. Mary, who is in a religious order, tells me it is in following a rule of life. Ann, who is in recovery, keeps connected in working the twelve steps. My fundamentalist friend, Jane, tells me that she finds peace in reading and living the Bible. Susan, another Christian friend, tells me to believe in Jesus Christ and live by his example. My Jewish friend, Sara, tells me to live by the commandments and do good. Jodi, a friend following Eastern traditions, tells me to meditate, contemplate, and empty myself. Saddaf, my Moslem partner at work, tells me to pray regularly, fast, do good works, and at least once in my lifetime make a pilgrimage. My daughter tells me I will find my path in Nature. Jo finds God's voice in dreams. Jane and Diane find God by doing charitable works. Where are you, God?

I am learning that there are many paths to You. I have seen You are in the lives of all these friends who follow You by their many paths. I know there are also other paths to You that I am not aware of. You do not limit yourself to one way as we do. Your classroom is as big as our world and hopefully even more.

Be open to the many classrooms where God will choose to speak to and teach you today.

Psalm 28

**"Hear the voice of my supplication,
as I cry to you for help,
as I lift up my hands toward your most holy sanctuary."**

I visit a family member this weekend I have had great difficulty dealing with for many years. Her world centers on herself and what she wants you to do for her. I am powerless over this person. My worst character defects emerge from hiding as I try to relate to her. I want her to be different. I still carry resentments for what she was not able to do or what she did do during the many years I have known her since I was a young girl. I have great difficulty finding anything positive about her. She is dying. Another family member goes with me because we both have such difficulty being with her alone. We visit out of guilt and a sense of duty to see her before her illness reaches its peak. We stay with another relative who also helps us through the weekend. It turns out to be the best time I can remember spending with this dying difficult family member. I go with a great deal of prayers from friends as well as my own. My friends and spiritual friend tell me to go with no expectations. They remind me of the Serenity Prayer which suggests I have no hope of changing someone else, only myself and my reaction to that person. I know she is dying and there is no time left for her to be different. They tell me to accept her just as she is but set boundaries. When she asks for something, I tell her what I can and what I can not do. I also spend time with her in small increments. We meet with her, have lunch or dinner, and then take her back home for her, as well as us, to rest.

Our dying relative has had someone come in for days before our visit getting her apartment clean. My mind flashes back to many years and many visits in the past. I remember how spotless her home looked when I came to visit her. I remember how honored I felt that she wanted everything to look elegant for our time together. I suddenly realize that this is her sign to me of how much she cares. On this visit she does not seem as demanding or as out of touch with reality as in the past. Has she really changed--or are we the ones who have changed? Probably some of both. I only know that by some miracle now I relate to a difficult person in a different relationship. I almost see her as a person rather than an obstacle in my life. When I want to believe in miracles and answers to prayer, I will remember this weekend where God transformed a family.

Pray for acceptance for situations (people) in your life that you can not change. Pray for the knowledge to be able to accept them with boundaries and few expectations.

Psalm 29

"The voice of the LORD is over the water;
the God of glory thunders,
the LORD, over mighty waters.
The voice of the LORD is powerful;
the voice of the LORD is full of majesty."

I am literally running late. I am trying to get all my work done before leaving town and driving to our church's conference center for a retreat. I am trying to find closure for all my problems. I don't want to leave a dirty house. The plants need watering. There are phone calls to make before I can leave. I have a lecture I should finish. I have already missed the silent part of the retreat. Finally I say, "Enough. If I don't stop now I will miss the whole weekend." I throw my luggage and my harp into the back of the car and I speed out of town. I soon notice a sheriff's car with blue flashing lights behind me. I have never been stopped by the police before, and it takes me awhile to figure out that he is following me! I have a hard time finding a place to pull over. I get out of the car. I am met by an overweight Spanish-American sheriff speaking broken English.

"Lady, do you realize you were going 60 mph in a school zone? You need to be more careful when children are around. I had to follow you for several miles before you pulled over."

"I am so sorry," I meekly reply.

"When was the last time you had a citation?"

"I've never had a ticket."

"Well, I am not going to give you a citation this time. But Lady, you need to slow down and be more observant of your surroundings."

This man gets my attention. For at least the rest of the weekend, this strong, kindly sheriff will be my image of God standing before me as I try to slow down on this journey and be aware of my surroundings.

Pray that your life and my life can be lived at a different, slower speed. Pray that we will both hear the voice of God calling us to a different life.

Psalm 30

"I will extol thee, O LORD, for thou hast drawn me up,
and hast not let my foes rejoice over me.
O LORD my God, I cried to thee for help,
and thou hast healed me."

He didn't say goodbye when he left this morning. She didn't call today as she said she would. They didn't invite us to the dinner party. I was ignored when I walked into the room. I was left out of the program even though I put so much work into it.

Some days I have high expectations of how I want my family, friends, and those I work with to treat me. If they do not show me attention and love, I am hurt. Other times I accept them for who they are and love them for who they are without strings or needs from them, and know I am not the center of the universe. My spiritual friend tells me that my relationship to others is dependent on my relationship to God. When I feel loved and cared for by the God of my understanding, I do not need this constant attention from others. When I am not connected to the love of God, I reach out and expect it from other people. I am learning I cannot expect others to love me the way God does. When I ask for and demand that kind of constant love from others, our relationship is devastated. When I become hurt, when I feel someone is not caring for me as he or she should, I am slowly learning to take this as a sign that I may be off-track with my relationship with God rather than that person. When I am freed to be in relationship with that friend just as they are, not as I expect or want them to be, I again feel the peace of God — and I am able to share that love and peace more easily with them.

Pray for relationships with others—friends, children, spouses, parents, partners. Where you are asking them to give more love than they seem able to give, pray that you may feel and receive that love from God.

Psalm 31

"I have passed out of mind like one who is dead...
My times are in your hand."

This morning I remember friends and family who have died, recent and past. I remember a much loved judge from our congregation, a talented physician, a priest who treated me as if I knew what I was doing, the husband and the father of choir members, two neighbors from my hometown in Virginia, a forty-one-year-old daughter of a friend, a close friend's mother, the grandson of a member of our church, two older friends from my home recovery group I have met with for years, an associate in a religious order, a friend's long-time companion, and an unborn child. I feel so grateful for knowing the two older gentlemen in the small group. I now realize I may have known them best. Each week I would hear them talk with much humor about their own walk with God in times of trial and great joy. I knew my neighbors from Virginia during my growing up years. Paul lived next door and was the model neighbor, cutting the grass and often looking after the widow across the street who was at least fifteen years older. Frieda had survived her husband's death, living alone for over forty years, breast cancer, and a broken hip, and still had a love and lust for life. Ironically these two neighbors died within a few days of each other. Kay, my forty-year-old friend, died of a brain tumor. Actually I knew her mother better, since we had served together on a Cursillo team. I cannot imagine the pain of the loss of a child, even when she is in her forties. The last is the lost child of an old friend I journeyed with through her miscarriage. We both still grieve for the unborn, unformed. I know we both will carry this pain to our own graves. This morning I imagine my friends from my 12-step group comparing notes with the priest and the judge. I see Paul and Frieda being a good neighbor to Kay. I see Kay and the physician both caring for the unborn. I see the saints doing what we are and were unable or incapable of doing on this earth. Bless them all.

Pray for those who have died. Give thanks for the many ways they brought God into your life.

Psalm 32

"Then I acknowledged my sin to you,
and I did not hide my iniquity;
I said, 'I will confess my transgressions to the LORD,'
and you forgave the guilt of my sin."

I go to the hospital to pray with a group of friends for one of our friends who is dying. One of the women there is someone I have not seen for some time. She is someone I have needed to make an amends to for something I did over twenty years earlier. I tried never to let my drinking interfere with my work. I never drank when I was on call. I remember well that night I was not on call and drinking when our surgeon called me to come and perform a test on this person's daughter to determine whether she needed surgery. The surgeon told me, "I know you are not on call, but you are so much better than your partner who is on call." Well, of course I went in. My husband drove me in while I drank coffee all the way. I performed the test and told the surgeon that the little girl needed surgery. She went to surgery, and they found nothing. For years I have wondered if I would have done better if I had not been drinking that night. It is still eating me inside. My experience is that God will continually put people in my path that I must make amends to until I take some action. As we leave together and are alone, I am given the courage, and I tell her of the wrong I have done to her family. She lovingly dismisses it and asks me to pray for her family. I feel some relief, especially as I keep her family in my daily prayers. She lovingly gives me an action that is transforming my guilt to compassion.

There is still a part of me that is embarrassed that someone else knows my imperfection. The freeing part is that my mask is coming off. I do not have to pretend to be something I am not. I am freer to become the person God intends me to be.

Pray that God will give you the courage to make amends to someone for something that is still destroying your inner self.

Psalm 33

**"The counsel of the LORD stands forever,
the thoughts of his heart to all generations."**

Two dear friends in a relationship are in much pain. Both are also professional counselors. They have helped so many other people in trouble, but they cannot help each other. They can not apply in their own lives the basic techniques they both are experts in helping others work out difficult relationships. I am continually amazed how I as well as others can help others, but are blind to the same situations in our own lives. The solutions to problems in others' lives are often so obvious. We are more often clueless to what is going on in our own lives. Are we simply blind or do we feel we are so different, above the rules that others should play by? I don't know. I know we can so easily see the speck in our neighbor's eye but miss the boulder in our own.

How do we become aware? I usually see what is going on in my life by seeing it first in someone else's. It becomes a secondhand experience that I finally see as a firsthand experience in my own life. This realization often comes by talking to a spiritual friend. Someone asks for my advice in a situation. As I try to make sure they have looked at all their options, I realize I am handing out advice that I need to hear myself. Sponsors in 12-step programs speak of this often. The advice they give those whom they sponsor is usually meant more for them.

Today as you listen and speak to friends, see if the counseling you might give to friends is what God really intends for you to hear in your own life.

Psalm 34

"Keep your tongue from evil, and your lips from speaking deceit."

I go to a 12-step meeting on honesty. I have considered myself above all, an honest person. Each day as I take personal inventory, I see this is not true. Every action, every response I give is to ensure that others see me in a good light. I don't want others to think poorly of me or think I may be imperfect. As I am leaving the meeting, someone I did not know speaks to me, "I guess you must get back to work now at the hospital." I reply, "Of course." It is not true. It is my day off. I am not going back to work, but my image of myself is a hard worker, and I didn't want that image tarnished. I lie to a perfect stranger whom I may never see again to preserve my mask of someone who works so hard. I can not remain truthful even for a few minutes after spending an hour talking about honesty.

I do not know if dishonesty is something learned or is it innate to the human condition. I know it is at the core of my being. I daily struggle to adhere to the truth. When I fail, I know I must make amends or the pain becomes unbearable. I am not sure if I am becoming more honest than in the past or just becoming more aware when I am dishonest. Now I feel a sickness in my stomach when I do not tell the truth. This did not happen previous to recovery. Stretching the truth to accommodate my own needs and goals seemed justified. After all, my case was different.

When I am tempted to lie about a situation, I hope I can remember the pain that will eventually follow. When I do fail, and am dishonest, I pray that I will find courage to make amends.

God continues to give us another chance when we fail. It is another day. I am asked if I have finished a project that is past due. My modes operandis in the past would be to make many excuses, half truths, "I was sick, my computer is broken, I got the deadline mixed up." Today I tell the truth, "I am not finished." That feeling in my heart of being truthful is more satisfying than that sickness in my stomach when I am not honest. I want to remember the freedom I feel when I resist the temptation to be dishonest and tell the truth instead. I think this is not perfection, but progress.

For this day be observant of when you are untruthful. Try to make amends when you are dishonest, just for this day.

Psalm 35
"How long, O LORD, wilt thou look on?
Rescue me from their ravages, my life from the lions!"

I have a very difficult day at work. I come home exhausted. My partners had other duties this afternoon and I had to cover several jobs for several hours. I did not do well. I felt out of control. I couldn't answer the demands put in front of me. I had to make decisions quicker than I wanted to without much thought. I felt alone, trapped, carrying the burden of the world and there was no one to help me. I was in charge and not doing a great job. When the day was over, I came home very angry that I had had to do more than my share.

I am learning that when this anger comes up, I meditate on it, breathe it in and out of my body, and pray that I may learn some lesson from this difficult experience. I go to a meeting, talk with friends, have a good dinner, and then sit for a while. The answer slowly came. This experience had taught me what it is like for my partners to cover for me when I am gone. I travel a great deal and have many administrative meetings while I am at work. I always felt that what I was doing was so important that my partners should understand. I know at times they have been resentful of the time I have taken from my work. Now I know why. I often left them with a heavy burden while I was doing my "important work."

The next morning I read a passage in *When Things Fall Apart* by Pema Chodron, an American Buddhist nun. She describes patience as the antidote to anger. She tells us not to "white knuckle it" but to look at the unpleasant situation, chew on it, smell it, and see what can be learned from it instead of reacting to it. When awareness comes we can channel that energy generated by anger to a more useful purpose. She describes aggression as the opposite of patience.

Aggression calls us to fill the space immediately and react. She had mirrored my experience and the antitoxin that had worked for me. Now that I have some awareness, I hope I can change. I want to change. I will put it in my prayers.

If you become angry today at a situation, be patient with it, stay with it, and pray that you may learn some lesson from the experience.

Psalm 36

"Your judgments are like the great deep;
you save humans and animals alike, O LORD.
How precious is your steadfast love, O God!
All people may take refuge in the shadow of your wings.
They feast on the abundance of your house, and you give them drink
 from the river of your delights."

I meet with a woman who is trying to recover from her addictions who just doesn't seem to get the program. She has tried to work a program of recovery for several years, but keeps going back to her old lifestyle. She infrequently goes to recovery meetings. She does not speak to others at meetings, isolates herself, comes late, and leaves early. I have tried several techniques to change her behavior. I alternate between calling her frequently and leaving her alone. I obsess about how poorly she is doing and what an ineffective friend I have been. Her shortcomings are so obvious to me. The only consistent relationship I have had with her is that I keep her in my prayers. This is just by habit. Then suddenly after several months she is back at recovery groups reaching out to people as she never has before and has become more regular than the regulars at meetings. She goes up to new women, talks to them, gives them her phone number, spends much time with them. I have no idea what has brought about the change. I know I had nothing to do with this, for I had all but given up on her. I realize that I am not in charge even of the people I have been asked to help. Results are not up to me, but occur in God's time. When I ask her what has brought on the change, she cannot explain it either. When all else seems to fail in relationship, prayer still seems to work. My prayer is that this God will continue to change me as God has dramatically changed my friend.

Continue to pray for those in need even when your efforts to reach out to them seem to fail. Image them as an offering for the care of God. Surrender them to God.

Psalm 37

"I have been young, and now am old;
yet I have not seen the righteous forsaken or his children begging bread.
He is ever giving liberally and lending,
and his children become a blessing."

I am constantly told to turn my problems over to God for God's care and guidance instead of obsessing about them myself. How do I do this? I was brought up to try to fix a problem as soon as it develops. If there is a problem, if I try hard enough, I can solve it with hard work and perseverance. Experience has taught me that this is not the truth.

The greatest challenge for me is to turn over to the care of God the care of my children, all of whom are now grown. When I see them in difficulty, I want to step in and fix it. I constantly worry about decisions they make. I have difficulty allowing them to make their own mistakes. But who has appointed me with so much knowledge that I know what is best for the rest of the world, especially my children? When I have difficulty turning my children over to the care of God, I imagine a guardian angel that God sends to be there to protect them. I especially think of their grandmother and grandfather, their Nana and DeDe, who loved them so much. They have been dead for over ten years, but I still feel their presence. I imagine them with them, caring for them, loving them, and protecting them as I no longer can. I can remember the love of their Nana and DeDe caring so unconditionally for their grandchildren—and then I have a tiny glimpse of the love of God protecting and caring for all children... and all of us.

Remember loved ones who have died who may still be loving and caring for you and your loved ones.

Psalm 38
"My wounds grow foul and fester because of my foolishness."

I have notes written by this Psalm in my Bible about a conflict I had several years ago with a co-worker. Today I cannot remember any details of the crisis, but I remember it consumed my life at the time. The Psalm was a great comfort during that struggle. It helped me realize I had a part in the conflict. The Psalm is a comfort today. I realize crises of today will be barely remembered or even forgotten in no time. One friend often suggests to me when I am obsessing about an issue to write down what is bothering me, put it in an envelope, and open it a week later. When I later open the envelope, the crisis is usually passed or no longer has the power over me it did at that time. Also there usually is a new conflict that has taken its place. I recall a suggestion from Barbara Brown Taylor. She suggests "imagining your crisis from the perspective of a rocket shooting up into outer space. How does it look from ten miles away? From a hundred miles away, where you can see the whole earth hanging in space like a blue-green marble? How does your problem look against the backdrop of the whole world?" I am gaining a little glimpse of God's time, not my time, and how God is constantly healing me if my wounds are open to this healing power.

When you are dealing with today's crisis, try to imagine how important this problem will be in your life one week from today, one month from now, one year from now.

Psalm 39

"I said, 'I will guard my ways that I may not sin with my tongue;
I will keep a muzzle on my mouth as long as the wicked are in my presence.' "

I attend a Benedictine retreat at Kanuga in western North Carolina. The quiet lake and cool forest are a perfect setting for learning about this spirituality. I only know one other person at the retreat. In the midst of the first day I find myself subtly trying to let people know who I am by dropping little remarks about what I do—playing the harp, writing, being a physician. I make certain that the one person I do know sees one of my books in the bookstore. I realize I have my self-esteem and identify tied to the "doings" of my life. I am so busy trying to let others know who I am that I am missing who they are. I am not looking for the Christ in them and certainly am not showing forth the Christ in me. This is an awareness of the day. I want to change. My prayers tonight are that I will change. More has been revealed to me of my character defects. Tonight I confess my faults and I turn them over to God for transformation. I believe that our loving God is in the business of transforming us if we will only be open to the change. Tonight I feel aware and open.

Meditate on one your character defects, sins of the day. Be open to God working in your life to change it.

Psalm 40

"Sacrifice and offering you do not desire,
But you have given me an open ear."

We meet today for coffee. She slowly walks into the café, sits at the opposite end of the table, and does not make eye contact for several minutes. We talk about how hot it is and how long it has been since we last met. Finally and slowly she looks up and begins to talk about what has brought so much immobility to her body and her life. She tells me how fear of hurting someone else has paralyzed her medical practice. She lives in such fear of doing harm that she no longer can care for or help her patients. I identify with this. I share how my prayer each morning also is that I will help and not harm a patient or a child. I no longer can perform certain routine examinations because I know they are painful even though I know they may eventually lead to healing. I share how I believe that my inability to cause physical pain is an outgrowth of my fear of causing emotional pain. I was taught in my early years that the greatest sin was to hurt or offend someone. This character trait has become an asset and now a great liability. I can be sensitive to others, but I sometimes cannot be truthful if it will offend. I cannot always be honest with my friends or loved ones or even my enemies. I begin to understand all this even more as I hear my friends speak of her fears. I am often blind or in denial to my own state until I see myself more clearly in another. We are both now more aware of our wounds because she risked intimacy. As we hug and leave, we both agree that some of the power of our fear to hurt has left our minds and our bodies. More and more each day I know that God calls me to community. This is where my healing will begin.

Pray for ears to hear the voice of God in the lives of others when you are blind and deaf to God's voice in your own life.

Psalm 41

"Happy are they that consider the poor;
the LORD delivers them in the day of trouble.
The LORD protects them and keeps them alive...
The LORD sustains them on their sickbed;
in their illness you heal all their infirmities."

We visit one of our favorite photography galleries during a trip to New Orleans. We are intrigued by Lewis Hine's photographs from the last century of children laboring at jobs that would have taxed adults today. Their thin haunting faces call out from the worn photographs with the same power they had over a century ago. As the shop keeper now handles the black and white photographs with white cotton gloves, we see four and five-year-olds picking cotton, standing on boxes and shucking oysters, working at cotton mills for twelve and fourteen hours. Their gray, expressionless faces are like forty-year-olds. These stark photographs were instrumental in changing the child labor laws in this country. Hine's art made a dramatic change in the social conditions of his day. I think of the still-abused children of our day: abused by their parents, abused by illness, abused by alcohol and drugs. I also think of the abused child within all of us: the child who had to grow up too fast, the child who did not know discipline with love, the child who is still hungry. All of these feelings are triggered by one man's art. My prayer today is that each of us will be touched by the creative spirit of God within each of us to reach out and to acknowledge the needs in the lost or abandoned places in one another by whatever art form is unique to us. Painting, writing, sewing, knitting, pottery, music, film, and recording are just a few. God has given us so many ways to speak our truth, to move from a life centered on ourselves. Speaking out is only one way.

Pray that the creative spirit within you will touch you to see the needs of others and be able to reach out of your own needs.

Psalm 42

"My soul thirsts for God,
for the living God.
When shall I come and behold
The face of God?"

Today I give thanks that I may have seen a glimpse of the reflected face of God. We are on the Alabama Gulf coast in Foley and stop at Stacey's Old Tyme Drug Store on Laurel Street. This corner drug store is a wonderful step back in time with a soda fountain and friendly hometown faces.

Stacey's reminds me of Riddle's, the drug store in my small hometown in Virginia that I walked to every day after school. Two stores up from Riddle's was my grandfather's jewelry store, where I would first stop to receive a nickel from my grandfather to buy an ice cream cone. In Stacey's there is an old time jukebox and a player piano along the walls that frame the front of the store filled with metal ice cream tables and chairs. To one side is a large metal box filled with cold bottled drinks. Behind the long marble counter and in front of the sparkling traditional drug store mirror stands John, the most friendly, most positive person I have encountered in some time. His cheerfulness, his caring for his customers, his striving for excellence in his shakes and sodas, and his reasonable prices are beyond comparison.

Observing someone who seems to love his work and loves people is like going to a museum to study a priceless work of art. We go there not only for a "shake fix" but also for a "feel good fix." John makes you feel good. He seems to love life and love people -- all kinds of people. As he takes your ice cream order, he makes eye contact and acts as if each of us is his only customer. He brightens your day with his big smile and upbeat remarks. "Welcome back to Foley! Isn't the weather great today!" He hands you a napkin and glass of ice water before he takes your order. "Our special today is the peach ice cream. One scoop or two? Cup or cone? Sit at our counter or a table and rest awhile." He makes you stop, rest, and look on the brighter side of life. He challenges you to lighten up, not be so serious. Of course he is the supreme extrovert, constantly talking, but even we introverts want to catch a little of what he has to offer—and it is more than a wonderful milkshake. His cheerful voice and smile are infectious. We always leave in a better frame of mind.

Observing John makes you realize what a difference one person can make in the attitude of a whole town, what a difference one person can make by blooming where he is planted, what a difference one person can make by reaching out in love to others in his own unique way, what a difference a person can make by his positive attitude in a job that many people would think mundane and uninteresting and unchallenging. Jungian friends tell me that someone I greatly admire may represent a shadow figure--a part of me which is under-developed but there for the asking. Today as I leave Stacey's Drug Store I take with me in my mind a wonderful role model with attributes of kindness, cheerfulness and an unbelievable positive outlook on life. This image I saw reflected in the drug store mirror seems to fit one of "the many faces of God" I have encountered in this walk we are taking together through the Psalms. How exciting to meet that image face to face. Tonight as I review the day, I give thanks for the unique opportunity to be with a role model who has something I want to have in my life as well.

Spend time today with someone you admire who seems to possess a positive outlook on life. Tonight give thanks for that person as a role model.

Psalm 43

"Why are you cast down, O my soul,
and why are you disquieted within me?
Hope in God; for I shall again praise him,
My help and my God."

I do the very thing I do not want to do. I have vivid memories of going to 12-step meetings as well as glorious church services during Holy Week or Easter, walking out of church feeling serenely peaceful, and finding myself seconds later yelling at my children in the car as we leave the church parking lot or on the return home. Yesterday I went to morning prayer, exercised, went to a 12-step meeting, had lunch with a friend, attended a memorial service for a dear friend, and then went to work. As soon as I was there, situations started occurring that were not to my liking. My computer would not give me my email. Doctors were asking me to perform examinations I thought were not appropriate for their patients. Other physicians were not treating me with respect I thought I deserved. My ego was attacked and I soon reacted. All the peace producing activities of the day were as if they had not happened. This morning I wonder if I should take another path. Do all these centering parts of my life really help? Friends remind me that I might have reacted even more outrageously if I had not done the peaceful actions. Am I constantly doomed to my ego needs? Do I always have to react to other's actions? Will I find no peace from the demons that seem to lift their heads when I least expect them?

I hear the voice of a monk I met at the Serenity Retreat at a Benedictine monastery who was also in a recovery program. He reminded us that we have a sacred wound. It is our woundedness that allows God to enter into our lives. Our humanness will always be with us. We do not go to some retreat or read a book or attend so many meetings or go to church and become instantly well. Our struggle is life long. It is "progress and not perfection." As I look back, I can see the progress. There are little moments when my life does not totally center on myself. I must turn over this longing to be perfect, to be like God. It is not the human condition. I must pray for patience to accept myself where I am and be grateful for the progress that has entered my life through my sacred wound, to be joyful for this new life, to be content, to be enough, and to be satisfied that I am just where I am supposed to be.

Today meditate on one of your character defects that is becoming less overwhelming. Be grateful for the healing that has taken place and for the progress you have made.

Psalm 44

"Why do you hide your face?
Why do you forget our affliction and oppression?
Rise up, come to our help.
Redeem us for the sake of your steadfast love."

There is one job that all of my partners dislike. It is usually not stimulating and takes a good hour out of the day. This weekend I did this job for one of my partners. Actually it was an amends. I had become compulsively absorbed in a task at work that I enjoyed and stopped covering the job that I was assigned to that afternoon. This partner had covered for me and did my work as well as his. I apologized and then asked if I could make some restitution by covering the less pleasant job, which he was assigned to that weekend. As I went to work the next morning I was filled with love for my partner, of whom I am obviously very fond. I also was filled with a strange love for the job I was doing. I was doing this work as an act of love for someone I cared for. It was the right thing to do. My whole attitude was changed about this usually dreaded assignment. I enjoyed it and I think I did a better job. I left hoping that I could go to work each day with this attitude—that I was performing an act of love, "the next right thing." My experience is that God continuously redeems me when I go astray as well as redeeming tasks that seem to burden me.

Pray about some job you are asked to perform that seems to be a burden. Pray that you may find redemption in that work that is "the next right thing."

Psalm 45

"Listen, O daughter, see and incline your ear;
forget your people and your father's house,
and the king will delight in your beauty."

We stop for lunch on the way to the beach at one of our favorite restaurants, The Revolving Tables, an "all you can eat" family style restaurant in the Old Mendenhall Hotel in a small town outside of Jackson, Mississippi. The food is placed on a large lazy Susan in the middle of each table which accommodates approximately twelve people. Everyday they serve down-home freshly cooked vegetables, rolls and corn bread, and catfish and ham the way your grandmother cooked them for Sunday dinner. You quickly learn the art of catching food as it whizzes by on the large lazy Susan at your table. Similar to a Japanese steakhouse, you may sit with strangers if you didn't bring eleven other people with you.

Mississippi has as many interesting people as Arkansas. This time we sit across the revolving table from the minister, his wife, a deacon and his wife from a local Baptist church. The minister's wife was very proud of her husband. When she introduced herself to the gentleman next to her, she made it very clear which Baptist church and how large a church her husband led. I immediately said in my mind, "Not another one of those! One more woman living her life through her husband."

Through the course of the meal, with true southern style, the preacher's wife related by eye contact with each one of us at the table. I waited my turn. I knew what to expect. I was anticipating that special smile I had grown up with, that look that I also knew how to emulate. But when it came my turn, as she replaced the creamed corn and butter beans I was waiting for, her smile was not that Pollyanna pious southern syrup I expected. When she looked my way, to borrow from Wesley, "I felt my heart strangely warmed." Her gaze was compassionate, not sentimental. It was an "I've been there, too" look. Her expression reminded me of the people in the last scene from the movie *Places in the Heart* when the peace is passed at another meal where all of the characters, living and dead, are now reunited in a common bond of love.

I do not know how you smile "the peace of God" to someone, but the preacher's wife expressed it to me. I felt her eyes, her mouth, her cheeks saying to me, "Namaztè: I see God inside you, and I rejoice in it." I suddenly remembered receiving that look often in my past from another preacher's wife, my grandmother.

We smiled at each other several times. I never introduced myself or heard her name. I don't know what this encounter meant to the preacher's wife, but I felt loved and accepted by this woman I will never know.

Here we were, two very different women in our goals, our lifestyle, and our relationship with God; and yet we were able to see, receive, and transmit God in each other. I felt a glimmer of hope that if two dissimilar southern women could accept each other, for a brief moment in time there was an expectation that we all might make a connection with God within each of us and maybe even expand it into several minutes or even longer. I especially felt hope that my judgmental prejudices might be healed and transformed by the God who made and loves us all.

Look for God in someone you least expect to find it today.

Psalm 46

"God is our refuge and strength,
a very present help in trouble.
Therefore we will not fear,
Though the earth should change."

Rosa Lee Parks lived with the injustice of segregation in Montgomery, Alabama. She wanted the earth to change. She acted against the injustice not by trying to make other people change, but by changing her behavior. She quietly decides to move one morning from the back to the front of the bus. Changing her behavior had earth-shattering consequences, but she had no control over the results. There must be many other African-American men and women who also dared to change their behavior to overcome injustice, but the results of their courage to change were not as immediately evident.

"Lord, grant me the serenity to accept the things I cannot change, courage to change the things I can, and wisdom to know the difference." Each meeting of many 12-step groups begins with a moment of silence followed by this, the Serenity Prayer. The prayer is one of the best mantra of what to do next, what is "the next right thing?" The prayer most simply states the tension and paradox of change. There are three parts to the prayer---acceptance, courage to change, and wisdom to know the difference. Life is like living on a balance or seesaw where wisdom is the fulcrum and acceptance and courage to change are at each end. Wisdom lets us know when we have gone too far to one side and need to put more weight into acceptance or into courage to change. Many people, more often women, have spent much of their lives on the acceptance end of the seesaw, feeling that they had very little ability to change their lives. Others have lived a life on the change end of the seesaw, trying to manipulate and change others into their way of thinking.

The wisdom of change for me has become: I can only change myself. I am most ineffective in changing others. This completely turns around the idea of change. When I am presented with a situation where I am trying to decide should I accept the situation or should I try to change it, I ask the question, "Does this involve changing me or others?" If it involves changing others, I go to the situation with a lot of acceptance. If the situation involves changing myself, I pray for the courage to change. Changing others is in the hands of God.

We are obligated to speak out our inner truth as articulately as we possibly can, but we have no control over how it is accepted by others. This does not mean that we are passive when we see injustice or violations of our inner truth. Our job is to articulate our truth with all the talents we can muster. However, we must go into a situation with the knowledge that the results are in the hands of God. My prayer today is that I will have wisdom to accept situations involving changing other people, but that I also will have courage when I realize it is my time to walk from the back to the front of the bus.

Consider making The Serenity Prayer a daily part of your life.

.

Psalm 47

"Clap your hands, all you peoples;
shout to God with loud songs of joy...
God has gone up with a shout."

When I was in high school, my dream was to become a cheerleader for the West Point Pointers. This was my image of acceptance. I tried out for cheerleading for four years and failed each year to be elected. I vividly remember my senior year when I lost at my last chance. I cried for days. I hit a new level of low self-esteem. I had prayed that I could be a cheerleader like my friends in the rest of my crowd. My prayer seemed unanswered. I felt unpopular, isolated, unloved. I often think that one of the reasons I went to medical school was to build up my self-image that was so devastated by not being a cheerleader. I am embarrassed that this seemingly trivial event should have been such a motivating factor in my life. I am comforted by Gerald May who went to a therapist when he worried that his reasons for becoming a physician were not "pure." The counselor told him the important factor was whether he enjoyed his work. God works in mysterious ways to lead us to green pastures and still waters.

God often answers my prayers in a completely different time zone than the one I am in. God's answer may be "yes," but it is often a radically different "yes" from what I prayed for. The answer is usually far removed from what I, in my "infinite" wisdom, ever imagined. Now, over fifty years later, I realize my "cheerleading" prayer has been answered. A major part of my work is being a cheerleader. My job as a teacher, a deacon, a parent, a grandparent, and a senior partner in my medical profession is to empower other people to see their potential. My job is to try to lead them to work that fits their talents and interests, to catch them doing a good job, to encourage them when they meet stumbling blocks.

God has led me, taught me, encouraged me to be a cheerleader for a different team from what I prayed for (and I don't have to shout or turn cartwheels or be coordinated or have a great figure). Thanks be to God![3]

Reflect on possible unrealized answers to your prayers -- better answers than you had prayed for. Give thanks for these answers.

Psalm 48

"We ponder your steadfast love, O God,
in the midst of your temple.
Your name, O God, like your praise, reaches to the ends of
the earth...
That you may tell the next generation that this is God,
Our God forever and ever,
He will be our guide forever."

We travel to Washington for a long-planned pilgrimage to the National Cathedral for Arkansas Day. It is glorious to worship in our nation's capitol with old and new friends from our home state. Early one morning our group is led by one of the canons of the Cathedral on a spiritual pilgrimage through the chapels of this magnificent house of worship for all people. The canon's words are profound. He talks to us about how to discern God's will in our lives. He tells us things I know I will never forget. He also shares some of his spiritual journey to illustrate certain points. After I return home, I try to write down some of the significant parts of his message. I have forgotten what he said! I can't believe I have forgotten his insightful words of wisdom. What is amazing, however, is that I can easily remember minute details of the story about his life. I remember the words of a friend who believes that the most important thing we have to offer is our story. He believes that our story is the most precious gift we can give to others. A basic premise in 12-step recovery is "sharing your experience, strength, and hope." I think of sermons I remember. I rarely remember the wonderful words of wisdom, but I always remember the stories. Is this one of the reasons that Jesus told us his message so often in parables? I begin to see the power of stories in other areas. The Bible is a book of so many stories about the relationship of God with God's people. I forget the laws, but I can remember the stories. How exciting to see one more way that God so passionately and personally speaks to us through the Word and through other people.

Share parts of your story with someone else today -- or even better -- ask another to share parts of his or her story with you.

Psalm 49

"I will solve my riddle to the music of the harp."

I love all the references to the harp in the Psalms, for this is my instrument of choice. I am an amateur musician, but the sound of the harp soothes my soul. It calms my spirit. It quiets the committee meeting in my head. I can visualize this happening in Saul's mind as David played. So many problems in my life have been solved by playing the harp. My obsession to answer problems on my own sometimes leaves me. My need for an immediate solution is quieted. Music allows me to feel something in my life other than the problem which is consuming me. I learn a little about waiting for the answer. It comes — sometimes in a dream, sometimes from a soul mate or friend in recovery, sometimes in a walk, sometimes in a reading, sometimes in the actual music, sometimes from a stranger.

The harp also heals the body. Music not only changes the mood of my mind, but I can feel the vibrations of the music from the instrument in my body. Muscles seem to relax.

Is this not true of all music? It is a sacred universal way of speaking to ourselves and to each other that has no language boundaries. Music is an icon for "something greater than ourselves." The vibrations, rhythm, pitch, tone of music also change and speak to animals, plants, perhaps all of nature. It may be our closest encounter with God language.

Listen to or play a musical instrument today. Contemplate it as a gift from God to help "solve life's riddles."

Psalm 50

"The mighty one, God the LORD,
speaks and summons the earth
from the rising of the sun to its setting.
Out of Zion, the perfection of beauty,
God shines forth."

My most spectacular sunrise was at Maui from the top of the volcano at Mt. Haleakala. I had to get up at three in the morning to make the ride up the mountain. It was dark, cold and very windy at the top. The spectacle was worth the trauma of the morning. The sunrise was breathtaking, indescribable. We were at the top of the edge of the world. The change from cold darkness to radiant morning was awesome. I can still see the multicolored sky and feel the warmth of the sun coming back to the earth.

Sometimes when I am dealing with a problem, I cannot sleep. Often I will channel surf the difficulty and solutions semi-consciously in my head as I lie in bed. I only find relief, however, if I physically get up, go sit on my porch and read or write or meditate in a more conscious state. I have watched many sunrises this way. I always find healing as the amber pink light of the new day begins. The new light is a constant reminder that the darkness will never stay. For eons the light has come back each day. The sunrise is like the rainbow. It is a reminder of God's constant presence and love.

Arise early enough this day to watch the sunrise. If you are in a period of darkness, visualize God's presence coming back into your life as the light comes back into the world.

Psalm 51
**"Create in me a clean heart, O God,
and put a new and right spirit within me."**

The Psalms our choir sings as anthems seem to be the verses I most remember. These lines from Psalm 51 to the music of Brahms have been playing in my mind these past few days. How does God create a clean heart within me? The awareness of a right spirit comes most often in the lives of other people. I am constantly amazed how I am blind to my own sins and character defects. I seem only to be able to see them in others. It seems to be the human condition.

It is early November. Today I go shopping at one of my favorite stores for early Christmas ideas. All the clerks are busy putting out their first Christmas stock. I cannot find what I am looking for and ask for help. The clerk seems annoyed and asks someone else to help me. She is overwhelmed by the placing and listing of her stock. I am annoyed. Shouldn't the immediate customer come first and the stocking wait? What is the real priority — is it the present customer or the ever-present stock? Both are important, but which should have priority? Then in my irritation, I suddenly see my own reflection. I am flooded with memories of this pattern of interaction with my own patients and their families in my work. I become consumed by my own agendas and projects and problems. My first priority should be to my patients and other physicians who call or come by for consultation. However, I often find myself irritated when my assignment or agenda or project is interrupted by a patient or by another physician if they were not on my immediate agenda. I pray that I will learn that what is immediately presenting to me may be a higher priority. Will I also learn to be able to stop a project without closure? I am slowly learning that the new agenda that presents to me may be God trying to show me a new path...God's plan trying to interface with my agenda.

When you are consumed with another's character defect, consider this may be your own defect as well.

Psalm 52

**"Your tongue is like a sharp razor, you worker of treachery.
You love evil more than good, and lying more than speaking
the truth."**

Making amends, realizing my humanness, admitting
that I am wrong is still one of my least favorite things I have to
do. It is the tenth step of any 12-step program—"Continue to
take personal inventory, and when we are wrong, promptly
admit it." Yesterday my partners made me aware of some of
my character defects. I was aware of them, but naively
thought that no one else had recognized them. I am beginning
to realize that if I don't own up to my defects on my own, very
soon someone else will make me aware of them. Believe me, it
is easier to admit to one's mistakes *before* they are pointed out
to you by someone else. I have tried to change my behavior
today. So far so good, but it is an old pattern. I will keep it in
my prayers. I expect my partners to come up to me today and
say, "Oh, you are doing so much better." This is an
unreasonable expectation. This is not the real world. I have to
try to change not for praise but because I know it is the right
thing to do.

I also made amends today to someone I had harmed
many years ago. I have over the years made many excuses—I
thought I was doing the right thing at the time. Because of my
actions, this person was forced to leave his job and this city. It
was not a simple mistake I made. My best thinking greatly
affected the life of this person and his family. Over the past
months, this person has come up in several conversations.
Remembering the events has made me very uncomfortable. I
knew I would only find relief by making amends to him. I will
always remember our conversation this morning. I could tell
the event was still painful for him, but he forgave me and has
found a new life, which he described as being better than

before. I will always remember this kindness from someone I have wronged. My prayer is that I hope I can react with the same kindness to someone who has wronged me.

Pray that we will be given the strength to make amends to those we have wronged.

Psalm 53

**"God looks down from heaven on humankind
to see if there are any who are wise,
who seek after God."**

Huston Smith describes part of Jesus' uniqueness as one who cared not about what people thought about him but rather what they thought about God. This concept has haunted me, for I desperately care about what other people think about me. Do they like me? Do they respect me? My persona and others' perception of my persona are very important to me. I even want people whom I am in conflict with to like me. I am presently obsessed about someone I work with whom I think does not like me. It is an illness that I am becoming more aware of, and I pray daily to be healed of this need to be liked and glorified by all.

What a wonderful example God has given us of how to let people know about our Creator rather than spending time worrying about what others think of him. I see Jesus' teaching about God's love and his and our need for this love more in his action than in his words. He tries to transmit that love to each person he meets. He tells stories, listens to their stories, walks with them and dines with them, and his words heal them. Those in recovery talk about 12-step programs as being a program of attraction, not promotion. They are attracted to the program because they have seen how it has changed others, not because of the multimedia promotion campaign about it. I think this is also Jesus' example. If only I could see my job as being a vehicle to pass on this tremendous love I have been given rather than spending so much time worrying about what other people think about the vehicle.

Pray for an awareness of God's love that will allow you to reach out and love others rather than being obsessed about what others think of you.

Psalm 54

**"Hear my prayer, O God;
give ear to the words of my mouth."**

One of the most moving moments of a 12-step meeting often is its ending as all who have listened and shared for an hour join hands together and say the Lord's Prayer. I have also been deeply moved by three who have prayed this prayer that God has led me to in past years. I think of them each time I say the Lord's Prayer. All three were people I went to minister to and all three instead ministered to me. I went to pray with them and they instead taught me how to pray. I went to touch their hand, and instead I was touched by God within them.

My first visit was with a friend in recovery dying of cancer. As I was leaving I asked him, "Shall we pray?" I knew immediately we both desperately wanted to. We sat in silence and then he began the Lord's Prayer. Each visit was the same. We ended by holding hands and praying the Lord's Prayer. Now several years later I still think of Bruce or maybe I even feel his presence each time I pray our Lord's Prayer. They are the words to say when it is too painful to say anything else. I think it is God's prayer, and he or she is praying it for and with us.

My second visit was with a renowned speech teacher who shared our pew at St. Mark's, our local church. She was recovering from a devastating stroke. Her meticulous speech was often not understandable, but her will to recover was like none I have ever seen. When we first visited, it was evening and we said Compline, an evening prayer service, together. Her words were like another language, but when we came to the Lord's Prayer, she was even more determined. I could understand her first words— Our Father.

Several weeks later on our next visit, almost as soon as we embraced she brought out a card for an abbreviated service she had been saying with our minister on his visits—and she pointed to the Lord's Prayer. We said it together, and already so many more words were recognizable. Tears flowed from both of us. I can no longer say this prayer without hearing Marguerite. God spoke so clearly through her and her heavenly language.

My third visit was to another friend in a nursing home who had survived years of poor health with still the presence of joy. His speech also was changed, this time by surgery for throat cancer. He, too, was a role model of determination to live fully despite tragedy and loss of loved ones. He greeted me with a holy kiss and a look of love. He introduced me as his girlfriend. He showed me the latest travel books he had been reading. We said evening prayers —actually I said evening prayers. But when we came to the Lord's Prayer, his beautiful guttural, earthy speech boomed above my softness. There was God, suffering and loving and giving praise in that nursing home. As I left, I asked Mr. Carstens to pray for me. [4]

Pray the Lord's Prayer today and listen throughout your day to see if it keeps speaking to you. Consider keeping this prayer in your daily prayers in the morning, at noon, or at night.

Psalm 55

"It is not enemies who taunt me-
I can bear that;
it is not adversaries who deal insolently with me-
I could hide from them.
But it is you, my equal,
my companion, my familiar friend,
with whom I kept pleasant company;"

I have two friends who are fighting for their lives against breast cancer. Both have had bone marrow transplants, rounds of chemotherapy, radiation, and surgery to attempt to be cured of their own cancerous cells. I think of them with this Psalm. A part of their body, their familiar friend, has turned on them. They cannot escape or hide from this part of their being. They have kept pleasant company with their beautiful bodies and have often enjoyed a good life. They are seeking outside sources as well as other parts of this whole body for recovery. I can only imagine this struggle.

Those in 12-step groups also talk of addictions as familiar friends who have turned on them. We use our addictions—food, alcohol, work, drugs, other people—to allow us to cope with the stress of life. They work for a while, sometimes a long while. But eventually they turn on us and do more harm than the original stress.

Pray for friends whose bodies and minds and hearts are struggling with disease and addiction.

Psalm 56

"In the day I am afraid,
 I will have confidence in God...
You take note of my roaming;
 put my tears into Your bottle;
 are they not in Your book?"

A physician calls to request that I visit one of his patients who is just moving from the Intensive Care Unit (ICU) to a private room. He miraculously has lived through acute liver failure from his alcoholism. The patient is a priest whom he describes as a kind, gentle man, but a "raging alcoholic whose walk with death was ever so close." The patient's mother and an occasional clergy member have come for a visit. His physician thinks they have lost hope in his recovery and have given up on him. I still do not like to make cold calls but know it is what I must do. I remember that someone made a cold 12-step call to me and saved my life. I call the patient's room. No answer. I call the nursing station. The clerk answers, "Father Jim is in his room. He does not always make it to the phone. Come up and visit him this afternoon." I arrive, knock on the door and enter. Lying in bed halfway under a sheet is a pleasant man with a round, red face and bright yellow eyes. He seems annoyed that I am there. I say, "Jim?" He answers, "No, I am Father Jim." I make one step closer and reply, "My name is Joanna, I am a deacon in the Episcopal church, a long-time member of a 12-step group. Dr. Maloney asked me to visit you. He said he had received your permission for this visit." Father Jim responds, "Yes, I am a 12-step drop out. Did you bring a meeting schedule? I would like to return to the 12-step program, but I am tired and hungry right now. Could you call back and make an appointment?"

"Certainly," I answer. I leave my card with my name and phone number on his bedside tray. I slowly look back one more time as the door silently and slowly closes behind me. As I walk to the hospital parking lot I think about all the times of my "roaming" when people may have come to try to offer help to me, and I turned them away because they were not on my agenda. They did not have an appointment. I am gradually learning that God most clearly breaks into my life in a person, a place *not* on my agenda, in an interruption. As I turn the key and start the engine in my car, I pray that I can remember this for one more day.

When asked to visit or call someone you are not comfortable calling on, remember a time when someone made a call on you and perhaps reminded you what was important, or even saved you from your "roaming."

Psalm 57

**"I lie down among lions that greedily devour human prey;
their teeth are spears and arrows,
their tongues sharp swords."**

I have just received a yearly evaluation by my supervisor. Of course, I want to be perfect; of course, I am not. I realize so much about myself with this evaluation. I still do not respond well to criticism. I am depressed that I still am not doing well in areas where I consciously worked for improvement. I think I am unfairly judged in some areas. My superior's tongue is sharp; his words hit me like spears and arrows. More and more I realize how very difficult it is to rate and evaluate people. I know I am over-reacting, being too sensitive and taking the evaluation too personally. I will try to process this and work for progress. What can I learn from this? So much of my self-esteem is tied into my work and my job. If I am told I am not perfect, I feel I have failed. I am still having difficulty accepting myself as human. Sometimes my work becomes God. I know now that it will eventually fail me as a source of self worth. It is the "perishable wreath" that Paul talks about in Corinthians. My experience is teaching me that the only eternal wreath is my relationship to God.

I also hope I can remember this feeling of unworthiness and remember to try to evaluate others without putting them down. I share this feeling of low value with a friend and he tells me about a similar experience he has had with a supervisor. My friend and the Psalmist help me no longer feel unique or alone.

Pray to be more accepting of your character defects and seek progress, not perfection.

Psalm 58

**"Do you judge people fairly...
O God, break the teeth in their mouths;
tear out the fangs of the young lions, O LORD!"**

These "hate" Psalms sometimes repulse me. At other times when I am in touch with my real feelings, I identify with everything the Psalmist cries out for—revenge, bad things for those who persecute him. I have had great difficulty with a person I have worked with for over fifteen years, constantly working through resentments for how she has treated me and others. Sometimes when she has talked to me, my only chance of survival has been constantly to pray so that I would not feel the pain and unpleasantness she was sending my way. She never sought others' advice and seemed to thrive on putting others down at every encounter. She would sometimes talk in consultations as if I were not present. When I was around her I felt devalued. She treated many people this way. I always wondered what it might be like to be one of her patients. Did she treat them any kinder? Sometimes her unkindness was mixed with bad judgment, for she only relied on herself and her judgment. I often thought about how wonderful my life would be if she were not here or I would not have to work with her. She would be a good reason to try to find a job somewhere else. I often wished that she would leave. I have to admit to some murderous thoughts at the heights of some of our most unpleasant encounters.

Today she died from a long battle with cancer. I no longer work with her, but my life is not very different. Other people have filled her place with many of her same characteristics. I have learned that difficult people will always be with me. I can move away from one, but I will find another at the next job with usually a new little twist. I am learning that I must deal with difficult people where I am, learn what I can from the experience, try to set boundaries so they do not harm me, and try to find what is that part of them which I loathe which may really be a part of me. Interestingly, this woman is the one who pushed me into the area of my greatest research interest and accomplishments in medicine. How strange God directs us even through the most difficult people.

Pray for the difficult people you live and work with.

Psalm 59

"Deliver me from my enemies, O my God;
protect me from those who rise up against me."

I am listening to tapes of the Genesis stories in my car on the way to work. I am struck by the repeated hardships the biblical women and men deal with and how God always seems to care for them. I love the Jacob stories. Here is a man of my own heart who lies and steals, but God still cares for him. Jacob is also lied to by his father-in-law, but he continues to work for his beloved Rachel. He endures hardship after hardship. The stories do not speak of his grumblings. I think of Joseph, who endures great adversity that later turns out to be a blessing. Could I survive being rejected my all my siblings and sold as a slave, taken to a foreign land, falsely accused, imprisoned, and forgotten by those I helped? His endurance leads to the salvation of an entire nation. I think of my own life. I often feel I have been dealt an unfair blow or a dirty hand. None of my difficulties, however, are as great as those of most of the biblical stories. My experience is that if I ride through the hardships and continue on, God will care for me, and some blessing will become evident. My experience and that of our biblical ancestors is that God cares for us and leads us through repeated difficulties. What I think of as hardships may later turn into blessings. My mind is not that of God's. I need to read Genesis more often.

Read the Joseph story. Are there similarities in your life? How might God be talking to you (whispering, shouting, singing)? Write your own version of the Joseph story, whether based on your own life or someone you know.

Psalm 60

**"Give victory with your right hand, and answer us,
so that those whom you love may be rescued."**

Tonight as I say my prayers, I am still physically present at a healing service I attended earlier in the morning in the Bethlehem Chapel at the National Cathedral. That chapel is especially beautiful in the early morning. We literally heard angel voices as the new Cathedral choir for girls was practicing above us for their first Evensong in two weeks. From my back row seat, I watched people from all walks of life come in for a chance to begin their new day with a new life. Some were in sandals, some in high heels and business suits. Some hurried in late, others had been there praying when I arrived. As others knelt for the laying on of hands and the anointing of oil at the altar, I became more acutely aware that there was more pain in the world than my own. I felt connected to the pain and suffering of my brothers and sisters at that place. Then as the priest laid his hands upon my head, I felt the warmth of many other hands on my back. Others from the congregation were also laying their hands on each of us at the altar and silently praying for healing. I felt the warmth and strength of a community lifting me up, a community of those whom I probably would never know or see again. I still feel the warmth and strength of those hands on my shoulders and back today. This is my most vivid and literal experience of the physical presence of the hand of God. I pray that I may carry their strength and prayers with me and that in turn I may bring comfort and strength to another as that congregation did to me.

Reach out and touch a friend in need today, either literally, figuratively, or both. Pray for his or her healing.

Psalm 61

"Let me abide in your tent forever,
find refuge under the shelter of your wings.
For you, O God, have heard my vows;
you have given me the heritage of those who fear your
name."

My mother-in-law had been dead for over seven years. I went back to Memphis, her hometown, for a book signing of a book of meditations. When five of her old girlfriends found out, they were there bright and early at the bookstore. I had not seen them for many years. I remembered all of them well. They had been friends with Elizabeth for twenty, thirty, or forty years. I was flooded with old memories of hearing her speak about luncheons, PEO functions, and church meetings with them. Many had taught school with her in Memphis. I felt surrounded by their support, just as I know I would have been by Elizabeth if she had been there. But I felt her there. I felt her presence more than I had since she had died. Do each of us carry a little of the soul of each other? Or is it a mirror of each other's soul? Is it like the extra mantle which Elisha asked from Elihja when he died? I do not understand it, but I felt it. We talked about Elizabeth and the gifts she had left us. No one mentioned anything material. Her gifts were her enthusiasm and love of life. We remembered them. I had forgotten. We all left with a little more of her gifts to us than when we came. I felt rejuvenated. I had an awareness of love and gifts, which can still be given even after death. I think I had a little glimpse of an encounter with someone in eternal life.

Make a list today of those who have nurtured you, especially those who continue to do so even after their death.

Psalm 62

"How long will you assail a person,
will you batter your victim, all of you . . .
Their only plan is to bring down a person of prominence."

Does this sound familiar. Amazing how little the world has changed in thousands of years. The social commentary by the Psalmist fits well with the political scene of our last several presidential administrations. Millions of dollars are spent to find any possible wrongdoings by our country's leadership or those close to them. It has become a sporting event to destroy another's career. The wrong in these modern day witch hunts has become so obvious when people I know and have supported have been harassed. Does this also occur when the opposition is in power? If so, my prejudices often allow me to be deaf and blind to it. I hope I have learned to be more sensitive to this historical need to destroy those in power. It has become a national pastime, more popular than baseball. People spend hours in speculation and gossip about whether the president or his family or friends committed wrongdoings in different situations. It is as though we can ignore working on our own defects if we spend our time concentrating on finding defects in others, especially the prominent. It has become the most popular method of keeping those in power from carrying out their programs and ideals. They have to spend so much of their energy trying to defend the accusations. I also know from my own experience that someone with enough motivation and funding could destroy anyone else's career. No one is immune from some event from the past that could be used to destroy him socially or politically. We are all human and have erred many times.

How can we change the national hysteria of seeking out our leader's imperfection in order to keep them from accomplishing their goals of good faith? This is where I may finally be beginning to take action. I can speak out when comments are made that I know are untrue or half-truths. I can refuse to participate in the game. I can also encourage others and myself to be more in touch with our own humanness, our own mistakes. My experience is that the more knowledge I have of my own character defects, the more accepting I am of imperfections in others. In contrast, I also seem to become less observant of myself when I concentrate on pointing out the mistakes of others. I become less tolerant, more judgmental, less in touch with their and my own humanness. I am finding it is becoming pretty much a full time job for me simply to clean up my own side of the street.

Concentrate today on your own character defects, not those defects in others.

Psalm 63

"Because your steadfast love is better than life,
my lips will praise you."

I talk with so many men and women who have received messages from their childhood that they are not good enough. Often these messages have come unconsciously or consciously from parents. We do our best to overcome them — overachieve to win their love or prove them wrong, or give up and underachieve and become victims of our circumstances. Even when we are separated from these parental figures or they are dead, there seems to be some parental tape running in our head with the same message — "You are not good enough." That which confronts us on the outside has somehow moved inside. It might humorously be called a "parental trap." My experience has been that healing only comes when the God of my understanding has become that new parental voice. We no longer have to listen to those old tapes. Healing occurs with a new tape that comes with re-parenting from a relationship with God inside of us and God outside of us. The God of my understanding, the God the Psalmist speaks to, is the one who delights in us, thinks we are good enough, and loves us as we are. Peace comes when I know I am loved as a child of God. I do not have to achieve or perform. I am here to give thanks and praise for this constant love and simply be.

Three times today, tell yourself, "I am loved by God as I am. I am good enough."

Psalm 64
**"Hear my voice, O God, in my complaint;
preserve my life from the dread enemy."**

I have had the opportunity to walk with many friends with crises in their lives. At times of great pain they have often found spiritual acceptance and relief from their religious community and their relationship with God. When the crisis becomes more tolerable, they sometimes seem to lose that contact with the spiritual thread they had hung on to at the depth of pain. As I see myself passing judgment, I realize I am no different. I can always see the truth so much more clearly in the lives of others than in myself. My spiritual life becomes central in times of distress. I am almost constantly in conversation with and crying out to God as does the Russian milkman, Tevye, in *Fiddler on the Roof*. My life becomes a dialogue with God. I don't believe that God gives us crises to draw us nearer. I do believe, however, that this is the redemptive part or resurrection piece of crises—an opportunity to re-center our lives as to what is important, what is central, our relationship with God. When I am out of crisis, I can look back and see that it was an opportunity to re-establish relationship with God. When I am in crisis, I can only see what is directly in front of me. My prayer for you and me this morning is that we will hold on to at least a small part of that relationship we find with God in times of great struggle. May we not lose the relationship when we are no longer in such distress.

Pray today for those in crisis, known and unknown. Pray that they may know the healing power of God in their lives. Pray that this knowledge will become a part of their being.

Psalm 65

**"When deeds of iniquity overwhelm us,
you forgive our transgressions."**

A newsletter from the Benedictine monastery at Pecos speaks of the reciprocity of forgiveness. Forgiveness is a channel. The channel is opened by our learning to forgive others for wrongs done to us. When that channel is opened, we will somehow also be able to receive forgiveness for the wrongs we recognize we have done to others. It is a basic part of the Lord's Prayer: "Forgive us our sins as we forgive the sins of others." I can understand this today. I have wronged another. I have not stood up and spoken out for a wrong done to someone else. This is one of my most frequent defects or sins, or missing the mark, not speaking my truth when I see a wrong being done. Some call it the defect or sin of omission. I want to change. I want to be forgiven. I make amends to the person wronged. I speak to the person who wronged her and tell her the side of the story I know. I know my best hope of being forgiven is by making that channel as wide as possible by forgiving others as well. I talk to a friend in recovery about people who know how to push my buttons, my vulnerable wounds. These are the people I most often carry resentments against. She reminds me of my part, that they push my button, but I helped install the buttons when I was wounded by someone else. The buttons were installed for protection. It is now time to find a better protection in a surrender to God. As I am more aware of my defects and wounds, I am more motivated today to turn over the resentments I have for past wrongs others have done to me. Becoming aware of my own humanness has allowed me to see and perhaps accept the humanness in another.

Consider that this Psalm may be calling you to widen the channel of forgiveness in your life. Choose one person you have wronged and meet with them or write them a letter asking forgiveness. If you write the letter, send it if you can.

Psalm 66
"Make a joyful noise to God, all the earth."

I love to sit in the second or third row at the symphony. The sound is probably better farther back, but I like to see the faces that connect with the instruments. Sometimes I feel that I am almost a member of the orchestra. One friend describes our seats as close enough to see all of the wrinkles and the sweat.

The metaphor of the orchestra representing a spiritual community is a natural comparison. It is a "we" program, not an "I" program. Alone we usually make such a faint or often shallow sound, but in harmony with so many varied instruments the sound becomes awesome. The comparison between the inharmonious tune-up when everyone is playing his own thing to that first sound after the community is formed and the conductor leads is beyond words. I also watch members rest as their instruments are quiet in a particular interlude. Can I, too, rest my part at different stages of my life when my work or what I have to say should be the silence of letting others be heard? There are times when I must let others carry the melody. But we all have our chance again at the finale. No one will be left out! All can again make their glorious sound!

I was particularly moved one night by the first cellist who suddenly had a thirty-second solo in the midst of the movement near the end of the concert. Suddenly one member I had seen all night was playing the beautiful melody above the rest of the orchestra. It was a mysterious sound that rose and waned like a wave in less than a minute—and like the visit of a ghostly spirit, this sound faded back and blended with the orchestra as it had for the rest of the evening. It was as if someone I had often watched took on new power and presence and just as suddenly faded back to his old familiar position. I knew that if I had been the cellist, I would have been too nervous about my brief solo to concentrate on the beginning of the concert. I was impressed by his ability to be in the limelight for a brief moment and fade back as if it were as natural as breathing. Could I do that in my life? Once I have the taste of the "starring role" I think that is where I should be. My blending in the community with others seems second rate. This is particularly true when one's egocentricity is this need to be the star.

My prayer is to play like the cellist—to work in my community, my family, my work, my church, my recovery community to accept the brief solo when it is called for—but know that what I have to offer in relatedness to others in upholding the harmony of my community is just as important. I pray to stay in tune by listening to others with different and with similar instruments and to stay in time by looking to my conductor, God. I fear, however, that much of my sound is often like the cacophony at the warm up. Next year, perhaps, I will consider taking lessons.

Attend a live performance of an orchestra or musical group. Can you relate to how the musicians in this community have something to teach our community?

Psalm 67

**"May God be gracious to us and bless us
and make his face to shine upon us."**

This beautiful Psalm is often said or sung at weddings. A choir I once sang with frequently sang William Mathias' composition of Psalm 67, written for the royal wedding of Charles and Diana in 1981. I know I will always think of Diana and her beauty and her kindness to children and her love and joy for her own children whenever I read or sing this Psalm. I will also think of her funeral in September of 1997 — the haunting English music, her handsome sons, the beautiful lilies on her coffin, the bouquet of white tulips from Prince William and the small wreath of white roses with a card from Prince Harry saying "Mummy," the outpouring of love and flowers from people all over the world. I wanted so much for someone to reach out and hold her sons' hands as they walked with lowered heads behind their mother's horse-drawn coffin. I will think of Diana whenever we hear the "Song of St. Francis" also sung at her funeral as well as Elton John's "Goodbye, England's Rose." When I hear this music or see these flowers I am also reminded of other beautiful women I have known who are no longer physically present in my life: Earle, Gloria, Martha, Maggie, Miff, Nyna, Dodie, Elizabeth, Jane, Virginia, Sylvia, Peggy — I pray that God will be gracious to us who celebrate their lives and the legacy and example they left for us. I pray that God will bless us and fill us with the desire also to live a life of beauty and kindness and love for others as they did. It is our best way to honor the time they spent with us.

Remember and give thanks today for so many in your past who brought beauty into your life and taught you how to love.

Psalm 68

**"O rider in the heavens,
the ancient heavens;
listen, he sends out his voice, his mighty voice."**

I think I am doing well with some of my character defects, and then up roars one like some ugly slimy green monster from a deep unknown swamp, often out of control. One of my defects is the need to control and possess and hold on to people and things. I thought I was less attached to my possessions until this weekend when our children had a garage sale. As I looked into the carport, I saw clothes and possessions I had given them as presents. How could they do this? How could they sell what we had given them? My daughter came into the house when she had made a big sale. She enthusiastically told me how she had just sold her grandfather's television. "You sold your grandfather's TV!" I spontaneously blurted out. As I drove away that early morning to meet with friends, I began to realize what I had done. I had not given up these possessions. We had given them to our children, but I had left attachments. I had given them with conditions. This was their life; these were their gifts. I also gave thanks to how gently our Lord had been in letting me know I was on the wrong track. I did not hear from heaven a booming voice saying, "Shame, You are a bad person." Instead I heard a quiet urging, "You must let go." Of course, if I do not listen to those little murmurs, my experience is that they do become more thundering announcements.

Today give thanks for the many times that God has gently let you know you are on the wrong path. Listen carefully and daily to that still small voice.

Psalm 69
"O God, you know my folly; the wrongs I have done are not hidden from you."

Several times a week I review X-rays of children who have been abused. There are very specific X-ray findings that tell us that a child has been secretly harmed. The fractures are classic and almost only seen from abuse or non-accidental trauma. On the outside the baby may appear normal. X-ray vision allows us to see inside to scars on the toddler's bones which tell us that some awful and secret trauma has occurred. In my work I only see the physical harm inside the body of that child. I sometimes wonder what deeper emotional scars are also present.

Life on the surface is so different from life on the inside. Our job is to look inward into ourselves and others to the scars of the inner life which all our attempts at outer beautification hide. The scars are present in all of us. We may spend much of our life pretending they are not there, but eventually the pain is too great. Many of our addictions are our feeble attempts to cover up these inner wounds. That is my experience of what life is all about, looking at the inner scars of our lives whose wounds we have tried to hide with our addictions, taking off our mask, beginning to live life on life's terms.

Pray for healing of your inner scars, known and unknown so that you may go on with the life which God has intended for you.

Psalm 70

"Let them be put to shame and confusion who seek my life! Let them be turned back and brought to dishonor who desire my hurt!"

I have these cycles of not feeling appreciated or valued at my work. I want to cry out. I talk to a spiritual friend. I light a candle, look outside my window, and meditate. Three revelations come. My feeling of value and self-worth come from staying in relationship with God. God values us for who we are, God's precious children. We do not have to keep being validated by other people. I will probably still be working on this concept on my deathbed.

The second revelation is that like us, the people we minister to and work with are also very wounded. They cannot respond with the love and validation we ask for. They are like us. Their cup may also be close to empty. Their wounds are too painful.

Our call is to stop the cycle of wounding. If I respond with anger and hurt about not being valued by others, my anger is continuing the cycle of wounding. Some deep wounds that occurred, goodness knows how long ago, have been perpetuated through the years in all of us. It is time for us to stop the cycle, stop the wounding. Buddhist friends tell me to stop, sit, rest, breath in the hurt, and then breathe out love, not more wounding. My prayer for today is that I can let my body transform those wounds even for brief periods during this day.

Sit quietly today and breathe in the hurt you feel from one person. Take the hurt into your body, let your body transform it, and breathe out love. Consider if you have some part in the person's reaction to you. Keep that person in your prayers for the next 30 days. Make amends if necessary.

Psalm 71

"So even to old age and gray hairs,
O God, do not forsake me,
Until I proclaim your might to all the generations to come.
Your power and your righteousness, O God, reach the high
heavens."

One of my favorite aunts died after a more than 15-year struggle with Alzheimer's. I am looking at her picture from my father's last birthday party. She has her arm raised high on his shoulder. I know that it is where her arm is also today. I know she is also talking and singing up a storm to make up for those last years when she could not. On Ash Wednesday when I heard of her death, I also received a call about a friend who was going to the hospital for her first baby and had asked for our prayers. I knew exactly what to say. My prayers were that our creator would send my aunt's spirit to be with my friend and her unborn daughter to comfort and guide and sing to them. I know she was there, for beautiful Hannah Sophia was born the next night. Whenever I will see her, in years to come I know I will think also of my aunt.

I pray that my aunt's spirit will stay close to us. We Johnson women need her strength, her love, and her endurance. We would also appreciate a touch of her humor if she could spare it.

I am thinking today of the death of Elijah. I know she would remember the story well. When Elijah died, he left behind his close companion Elisha. As Elijah was about to be taken into heaven, he asked Elisha, "Tell me what I may do for you before I am taken from you." Elisha said, "Please let me inherit a double share of your spirit." Elijah responded, "You have asked a hard thing." But Elisha's wish was granted, and God left a mantle or shawl on the ground as a sign for Elisha to wear as a symbol of his spirit. I speak today for all the women my aunt has left behind. Our prayer today is that we will feel the shawl about us of her spirit—her love, her endurance, her humor, her strength, her song—until we meet again, face to face. We were so blessed to have been her family. May God continue to bless her and may God continue to use her for his grace.

Pray for a double share of the spirit of women in your family who have been important in your life and have died. Put them at the top of your gratitude list.

Psalm 72

**"He has pity on the weak and the needy,
and saves the lives of the needy."**

I am at a power meeting of all the "heads of state" of members of my medical specialty. It is a political event to connect to people in powerful positions, to influence them, to be seen with them, and make power moves. I sit at the final banquet with a physician and his wife I have known for several years. He is the chair of one of the most prestigious departments in the country. They are different. They talk about their lives with great honesty, not trying to impress us with their achievements. They are more interested in what is happening in the lives of other people at the table than expounding on their most recent positions and power. They ask members at their table about their lives rather than elaborating on their own.

A select number of resident physicians in our profession are guests at the conference. Most attendees ignore them, for they are not powerful people. This couple calls attention to a resident and his fiancée coming in late. There is not room for them to sit together so they are seated at separate tables. My old friends leave our table and go over and ask the resident couple to join our table for dessert. They introduce them to many others they never would have met. I remember others who did the same for me when I was a resident in training, taking me by the hand in a strange place and introducing me to people who were giants in my profession as if I was just as important as they were. This may have been the most important lesson I learned at this meeting. Life is about caring about people and making a difference when you have the opportunity, making someone else's journey a little easier, especially those who are not considered powerful or people who can not return the favor. Those who do this take a road less traveled. I want to get back on that pathway. I hope it is an infectious disease.

Consider that this Psalm may be calling you to take a road less traveled today by relating to people not because of their status or what they can do for you, but because they are people on this same journey.

Psalm 73

**"But when I thought how to understand this,
it seemed to me a wearisome task."**

I have been working on a project for over 20 years which at times has driven and consumed me. I stay with the project because it is stimulating and interesting. I want to solve the puzzle. The work for many years appeared to be pure research with very little clinical value. I knew I was not immediately helping patients. I could find an abnormality, but there was no known cure for it. The work has involved studying the blood flow of the brain with Doppler ultrasound in children with Sickle Cell Disease. One of the major complications of their disease is stroke. The ultrasound is a way of seeing abnormal vessels before the children have symptoms. Another physician who first told me about the use of ultrasound just completed a monumental study showing that strokes in children with Sickle Cell Disease can be prevented by blood transfusion therapy.

Now my small part of the puzzle has real practical significance. There is a possibility that a child with this disease can be identified by ultrasound and treated before symptoms of stroke develop. There were many times in my work that I was very frustrated. Many made fun or ridiculed our work. Others criticized my methods. I painfully learned from those who were critical, for often they had points that I needed to address. There were times when I was very discouraged. I sometimes thought that the years of work were useless. Now the usefulness of the work is beyond what I had imagined. People are coming and calling from all over the country to learn about our method. For some time my daily prayers have been that God will bless this work and somehow find a use for it. My prayers have been answered tenfold. A constant part of this process for me has been the presence of God holding me up when I was discouraged. At each low point, some little light would appear that would help me continue—a new finding would develop, one of our technologists would make a new observation, another investigator would call about his or her work. I would be moved by the illness of a patient I had not been able to help. I also began to have some realization that my work was not of my doing but a gift from God.

Pray that God will bless your work and use it for the benefit of others. Give thanks for the gift you have been given to enable you to do this work. Consider whatever work you do as a ministry and put it at the top of your gratitude list today.

Psalm 74

"O God, why do you cast us off forever?
Why does your anger smoke against the sheep of your pasture?
Remember your congregation, which you acquired long ago,
Which you redeemed to be the tribe of your heritage."

There are so many times we must disappoint God by the acts we perform in the name of our religion. My experience is that this may be especially true when we exclude others from worshipping. The God of my understanding is not one of exclusion. Recently I went with my husband to a friend's home whose mother had died the day before. In their tradition, friends and family go to the home for several days in the evening to say prayers for the dead. What a wonderful tradition to share the grief of a loved one in prayers in community at home. I was surprised, however, to find out when we arrived that only the men were in a separate room chanting these beautiful prayers. The women sat in the living room and talked. I felt excluded from the ritual and worship. This is another religion's tradition, a tradition which I had difficulty understanding. There were some beautiful parts of their ritual, however. My husband told me of the graveside service earlier in the day where family and friends tore parts of their clothes in grief. How wonderful to be able to physically express grief.

I told a friend about this experience. Jenny then shared with me an experience at a service from another Christian denomination. An exchange student from South America was living with them and she would take him to the Hispanic worship service. She would never take communion with him, however. One Sunday he begged her to go up with him. "It will be all right," he said. Jenny reluctantly went up to the altar and was handed the bread by the minister. The minister handed her the bread and then looked into her eyes and said, "You're not a member of this faith, are you?" Jenny said, "No." The minister took the bread out of her hand. As Jenny walked away, her exchange student broke off part of his bread and gave it to her. They both walked by the wine station without receiving. As Jenny told me this story, so many thoughts flooded through my mind. I again experienced that feeling of rejection, not being good enough for the church. It is so easy to point fingers at other traditions. Then I began to wonder was it possible that I also might be promoting some policy or canon or law that was excluding or rejecting others from God's grace in my own tradition. It is so much easier to see the splinter in my neighbor's eye. The Prayer Book of my tradition offers the Eucharist only to baptized Christians. Might those who are not baptized need the body and blood of God just as much? Is it a sacrament that is earned or available only to those who "think" they understand it?

Remember the times you have been excluded by the tradition of organized religion or other communities you are involved in. Feel the rejection. Reflect on the possibility that you may have treated someone else similarly in your tradition.

Psalm 75

**"...but it is God who executes judgments,
putting down one and lifting up another."**

A friend talks to me about forgiveness and judgment.
She tells me how difficult it is to forgive a family member who
has deeply hurt her. She tells me she has been given the image
of Christ on the cross. He, too, was violated, whipped, and
mocked. His answer was, "Forgive them, for they know not
what they do."

Familiar words, but I hear them with new ears,
especially the "for they know not what they do." I realize most
people with whom I am in conflict, people for whom I am
carrying a deep resentment, do not have a clue about their
behavior. They act as if they have no realization of the pain
they cause, as if the knowledge of the truth is too difficult to
bear. They do not know "what they do." They are
unconscious. Could I also be unconscious of harm I may bring
to other relationships?

I innately believe we do not desire to harm one
another. We honestly believe our behavior is for the best or in
someone else's best interest. We are acting unconsciously to
the real consequences of our actions.

When we gradually have faint glimpses of our sins
against one another, we often go through the same stages of
death to our sins which Elisabeth Kubler-Ross describes in
death to our physical bodies: denial, anger, bargaining,
depression, and finally, acceptance of the truth. It is not an
easy process to see and accept our defects. We have walls of
denial to protect us.

My experience also has been that sometimes the
magnitude of my sin is too great for me to see and accept at
one time. The knowledge of the pain I may cause would

devastate or destroy me. It often must be revealed in small pieces that I can handle.

Jesus tells us we are often unconscious to our sins. What can we do? Be aware of our unconscious state. I seem not to be able to see the log in my own eye, but can clearly see the speck in my neighbor's. That is my clue. When I see a defect in another, my first question should be, "Is this behavior also in me?" It may be months or years before I see through the denial. In the meantime I usually spend much time being angry at my friend.

When I see behavior in another that is harmful, I am also learning it is appropriate to tell someone that I may be harmed or another may be harmed by this action. The difficult part is doing this in love without judgment.

In my experiences involving forgiveness, I have found that the best way to learn how to forgive is to be more aware of my own humanness. As I see my sins and defects more clearly, I have become more tolerant of others. When I am most judgmental, I am most out of touch with my own sinfulness or character defects.

Our job is to help each other in community come to consciousness in the most loving manner possible.[5]

Pray for an awareness of your own character defects so that you may learn to forgive others. Pray to leave judgment to God.

Psalm 76

**"Glorious are you, more majestic
than the everlasting mountains."**

I have just returned from a mountaintop retreat—a time of quiet, solitude, peace. I fear that this peace is so short-lived. How can I hold on to it? My life is studded with spiritual highs, mountaintop and beach retreats. We need oases for refreshment to bask in the love of God, but how do we keep this peace when we are not on retreat?

Reminders. Anne Morrow Lindbergh wrote about this in *Gifts From the Sea*. She kept shells on her desk that reminded her of different meditations she had in her solitude at the beach. I can keep reminders of times I felt the presence of God by keeping a picture, a rock, a flower that reminds me of that time. I can keep a journal and write about these moments and keep a running gratitude list. I can listen to music or sing a song that brings me back to that peaceful time. After I last returned from the beach, I started listening to a CD of the waves as I wake up each morning.

Discipline. I long for programmed time of solitude in each day to read, write, pray, or listen as I am able to do on retreat. My day quickly becomes too busy, filled with a multitude of tasks to perform before I will allow rest. A dear soul-mate suggests that instead of trying to escape from this busyness that I pray God into my busyness! I would like to change my busy task-oriented life which is always reaching for some goal, but so far I have been unable to change. Can I work the Serenity Prayer and accept that I may not change? Like the runner in the movie *Chariots of Fire*, "Has God made me this way—for a purpose?" Instead of pretending I am something I am not or wishing or praying for something I am not, I pray to know myself and accept myself for who I am—a unique gift of God. May I be transformed by God's presence and may I allow God to use my uniqueness. I also pray that I do not use the gifts I have been given to excess so that they become defects.

Awareness and Confession. Peace does seem to come most readily with the acceptance of who I am, a person made in God's image with gifts and defects. I become most aware of my defects usually first by seeing them in another person. God constantly seems to throw people in front of me with a mirror to let me see the person I really am---manipulative, selfish, self-centered, controlling, consumed with ego-centric love. Finding peace by becoming the person God created me to be comes most readily when I am made aware of these character defects and then letting go of them with a confession of these defects in private or public prayer to God, to myself, to another, a minister, a 12-step spiritual friend, or another member of a 12-step group. I take off my mask of perfection.

Illumination. As I slowly gain some knowledge of my true self, I pray for enlightenment, feeling connected to God. Those in recovery see little glimpses of what union with God is like as they daily work these 12-steps. This illumination often takes place most clearly in community, hearing other stories, especially at 12-step meetings. Here we hear stories of how God constantly illumines the darkness in our lives—events we cannot explain, unexpected and undeserved love and forgiveness from friends and strangers on this journey, beauty we never knew existed, rainbows, sunsets which appear and disappear in brief moments. Our job is to stay open, aware, alert, for these occurrences and share this experience, strength, and hope with the rest of our community as we hear their experiences as well. Peace and acceptance then run through our busy lives like a gentle waterfall from the highest mountain.

Consider how you may encounter daily illumination, awareness, confessions, discipline and reminders that can bring the peace found at a mountaintop retreat. Some traditions would call this a rule of life.

Psalm 77

**"Your way was through the sea,
your path, through the mighty waters;
yet your footprints were unseen."**

One of God's treasures is Kanuga, a retreat center just outside of Asheville, North Carolina. It has been a mountain respite for children and families for generations, but my husband and I only recently discovered it through childhood friends. On our first visit there one autumn, I was immediately drawn to the beautiful lake reflecting the orange, red, and yellow leaves on the trees around this natural mirror. My busy mind was quickly quieted. Our cellular phone would not transmit through the mountains. We were protected from the cares we had left at home. As I sat alone rocking and meditating in a large rocking chair by the swimming area of the lake, I listened to the morning's stillness, only interrupted by migrating geese overhead. Just as I was leaving for breakfast, I stopped motionless in my tracks as I saw an unobtrusive, wooden sign at the water's edge. I went closer to make sure I had read it right. Written on weathered gray board were the words, *Please, don't walk on the water.* I took it as a personal message from God. This is when I get into deep waters over my head, deep trouble—when I try to play God, when I try to walk on water. I did not make the lake or the sky or the trees. Neither am I able to walk on the water. My job is to be observant, open to and grateful for the love and pleasure of God, and to serve God as best I can by returning that love to God, others, and myself.

Make a conscious effort not to try to walk on water today.

Psalm 78

"Things that we have heard and known,
that our ancestors have told us.
We will not hide them from their children;
we will tell to the coming generation the glorious deed of
the Lord,
and his might, and the wonders that he has done."

I live in a family of history buffs. Two of our sons majored in history and my husband's secret passion and bliss is studying and reading ancient history. Our dinner conversations are often a trivial pursuit of the ancient world. I also want my children to know about our own family history I have known or heard about. I want them to know about our ancestors and how they were taken care of just like the Israelites in the desert. I also feel a need to tell our own story. I want them to know about the car accident when I was in medical school one rainy January night in 1967. I had to drop out of school for six months, but the new class I entered is where I met their dad. My life is still limited by handicaps from that accident, but I rarely curse them. I could have been even more impaired. I also have had a realization that I was led from that tragedy into a new life. People in 12-step programs speak of the same experience — the tragedy of their addiction led them to a new life, never realized. The miracle is there, already happening, waiting to happen. We must see it, tell it — and for some reason, we will forget it if we do not tell it over and over again.

Share with a family member or friend the miracles in your life.
Put these miracles at the top of your gratitude list today.

Psalm 79

**"Let your compassion come speedily to meet us,
for we are brought very low."**

How do you comfort someone in the depression and despair of the dark night of the soul? It is so awful, so painful. When you are in it, it is difficult to know or feel any reason. My experience is that only when I am out of the dark night can I look back and see what has happened. Sometimes the darkness is due to real clinical depression. Sometimes the darkness is a sign that one of my character defects is now in charge of my life. These are emptying times, times when my life has become filled with something that no longer works. In order to get out of the hole, I must shed some baggage, some part of myself, some character defect which has taken over. This shedding is so painful. It is like removing scales from a dragon to become a person again. One of the best descriptions of this change is in C. S. Lewis' *Voyage of the Dawn Treader*. A young boy Eustace has become so bad that he indeed is changed into a dragon. He has a moment of clarity and wants to become human again. Aslan, the God figure in the story, tells him to get into a pool of water and start pulling off the scales. Each attempt by Eustace to remove a scale is unbearably painful. Those caught in addiction would suggest one solution to Eustace would be to deaden or ignore the pain by using our drug of choice: food, alcohol, power, work, relationships. The solution of those seeking a life free of addiction would be to stay in the pool, ride the storm, often surrounded or held up only by the love of friends who walk or swim beside us. In Lewis' story, it is still it too painful for Eustace on his own to remove the scales which he now realizes represent his defects. Aslan jumps into the pool and pulls off the scales. We cannot on our own power remove the defects. Our job is to recognize our defects, confess them to another person and God, but only God can remove the scales. This usually takes time. The scab cannot come off before its time. A spiritual friend, Jane Wolfe, also tells us we need to stay in the recovery room as long as necessary after surgery for our character defects just as we would need to do for physical defects.

What sustains us during this time? The Psalms continually tell us that God promises to be with us, if we only have eyes and ears to see and hear. If our darkness is due to our character defects and we stay with the process, we can come out of the dark night a new person, healed by whatever God has removed surgically during that time of darkness.

If you are in a time of darkness, talk with a professional to see if you are having clinical depression. This is very treatable. This person may help you realize that a character defect is running your life. Talk with your spiritual friend and consider surrendering the defect.

Psalm 80

"Give us life, and we will call on your name.
Restore us, O LORD God of hosts;
let your face shine, that we may be saved."

My medical background tells me that life is breath.
My Christian background relates breath to the presence of the
Holy Spirit. Buddhist friends have taught me how to feel the
presence of the Holy Spirit in me by being aware of my
breathing. I have learned from these Buddhist friends a
technique of walking meditation. As I walk, I breathe in and
breathe out trying to be aware of only my breath. More than
anything else this has helped quiet the committee in my mind
so that I may listen and be aware and present to the moment.
This is my best way of waiting to hear that still small voice.
Practicing walking breath meditation outdoors also constantly
keeps me aware of a world much greater than myself, my
obsessions, my problems, my desires. The breath is Spirit—
God coming in and going out. When I concentrate on my
breath, I stay in the present, for my breathing is what tells me I
am in the present and very much alive. I am again reminded
of what C. S. Lewis tells us—that God meets us most likely
when we stay in the present moment, not in the future or the
past. It is where God intersects in our lives. When I am aware
of breathing, I am aware of the present moment. I also become
more aware of the wind, the sun, the birds, the trees around
me. Sometimes I observe plants and trees I have never seen
before, even though I have walked the same path for a decade
in the early morning.

I started this practice in my morning walk, but now I
have been trying to practice conscious breathing whenever I
walk—at work, at home, at the grocery store, at church, at
meetings. It has made all the difference in my life. My mood
changes to a slower pace. I become more observant of my

surroundings. Priorities change. Obsessions pass by like barges on a slow moving river. I become reconnected to something greater than myself and my thoughts.

Practice conscious breathing as you walk through your day.

Psalm 81

**"In distress you called, and I rescued you;
I answered you in the secret place of thunder;"**

Last night I sat and watched from a balcony as a thunderstorm moved up the beach along one of our favorite vacation spots on the Gulf coast. It was breathtaking. How in my over-sixty years could I have missed knowing this event? Storms have been a time to huddle in shelter, a nuisance for driving, a means of tracking dirt into the house, ruined hairdos, cancelled soccer games. From our balcony, however, we saw a panoramic view of night becoming day, white bolts flashing to the water, and awesome crashing sounds generating from emptiness. Two nights earlier, we watched from the same balcony a fireworks display from a nearby hotel, spectacular at the time, but now pale in comparison. I begin to know the power and awe of God. "Holy, Holy, Holy, Lord God of power and might, heaven and earth are full of your glory. Hosanna in the highest." I was afraid but awestruck. I sensed the transcendent God beyond knowledge. I felt power beyond knowledge. I felt power beyond myself and my world. Later, as I reflected, I realized the power of this electrical storm—and yet even this must be like a grain of sand compared with the omnipotence of God. I hope I can remember this night after I return home and find myself wrapped up in my own world where I live at the center. I hope I can remember this night and the gift of this observance of an unbelievable spectacular power much greater than myself.

Meditate on and remember times you have seen the majesty of God in nature.

Psalm 82
**"They have neither knowledge nor understanding,
they walk around in darkness."**

No matter what the topic is, many 12-step meetings eventually center on how people are seeking to turn their lives and their wills over to God. Many at the meetings are busy people who by worldly standards have been very successful, but still talk about a continuous search for what Christians call the "fruit of the spirit," a real peace in their lives. They share honestly about times their lives seem empty and times of peace and wholeness. Those who have glimpses of peace say the answer is through a spiritual awakening. At first this greatly troubled me, for I have felt that I was a somewhat spiritual person with some awareness of God working in my life, yet I only infrequently felt that peace. What was wrong? I am gradually receiving glimpses of truth. My relationship to God is sometimes like a visit from my grandmother. I deeply loved my grandmother, for she offered me so much agape, unconditional love. I would clean my house, I would prepare her room, I would so look forward to her visit. We would have a wonderful time when she arrived, and I would treasure the memories of that visit until we would meet again. I received letters full of unconditional love from her and gifts when I most needed and least expected them. We had a rare relationship that so many long for.

As glorious as this relationship was, God calls us to something more than being just an occasional honored visitor in our lives. God calls us to surrender, to be servants in the world, turning our lives and will over to the God of our understanding. I have only seen this peace I seek in the lives of people who are directed by God, not just visited by God. It is most difficult to move from my neat little world that I have worked so hard to arrange back to some less familiar world where I will surrender and be a servant, even when I have a glimpse that this God, this mistress or master, is one of total love beyond all my understanding.

I have difficulty comprehending being a servant, giving up control. These are foreign words to my way of life. My direction has been to be master of my own life, in control, making my mind and body perform any task my master mind has set out to do. Turning over control is difficult. I can, however, see myself as an infant or young child being loved and cared for in the arms of my loving and caring grandmother. I am helpless and completely dependent on her for love, and she does love me beyond belief. I see it in her eyes, her smile, her touch. I am not preparing the world for her visit. She has prepared it for me. She provides for my every need.

God does not want just to visit us. God calls us to a commitment beyond our understanding. When I am living in my addiction, I may have a relationship with God, but God does not direct or manage my life. God is not at the center of my life. I am still the director, the central character in the leading and directing role. I pray for change. I pray for peace. I pray to become as a little child, a young infant, completely in God's care.

Lord, I am going to be a tough servant to work with. Perhaps on your next visit you will teach me more. I am accustomed to my way of doing things. I would also like to stay in a nice place. I hope the job you have in mind for me is not too demanding. You know I am accustomed to nice things and being treated with respect. I know through my grandmother's love that you love and respect me. You are calling me to a love greater than I have known, greater than a grandmother's love. I cannot comprehend it.

Imagine being loved and cared for in the arms of the most loving grandmother possible. Perhaps it is your own grandmother.

Psalm 83

"O God, do not keep silence
do not hold your peace or be still, O God!"

St. Benedict tells us in the prologue to his rule of life called *The Rule of Benedict* to listen with the "ear of our heart." I long to do this. Usually when I am quiet and listen, I hear the murmuring of the committee in my head: "Do this, do that, you are not good enough, you may hurt someone, you will never get that done, this person is against you, stay busy, stay in control, push ahead." Esther de Waal speaks of changing the person to whom we constantly are dialoguing. Instead of dialoguing with this committee in my head, she suggests we dialogue with God. "God, what should I do next? God, where are you? God, should I try to accomplish this? God, how can this be?" I think she is calling us again to be like Tevye, the wonderful dairyman in *Fiddler on the Roof*, whose life was a constant dialogue with God. I am ready to try it. Listening to that committee of negative executives directing the inhabitants of the squirrel cage that goes on in my head has brought no peace. My prayer today for you and for me is that our conversation will be with God instead of the executive committee in our minds.

For today, make your dialogue with God instead of the committee in your head.

Psalm 84

"For the LORD God is a sun and shield;
he bestows favor and honor.
No good thing does the LORD withhold from those who
walk uprightly."

I continue to find peace in the techniques of walking and breathing meditations taught by my Buddhist friends. They teach me to breathe in love and breathe out peace as I try to put myself in position so that God will transform my life and the lives of those around me. Christian friends talk to me about faith and works, how both are important. Buddhist friends tell me to inhale thoughts of faith and exhale thoughts of works as I walk and meditate. Eventually, somehow by Grace my body will transform faith into works.

My Buddhist friends have also taught me when I am troubled to breathe in my pain and breathe out peace. I feel my pain. I don't try to avoid or anesthetize it with drugs or alcohol or work, but I allow it to be transformed and changed by the Spirit at work in my body into a more positive energy. They are also teaching me a little about getting out of myself, being "relieved of the bondage of self." They teach me about moving my meditation from my world to a larger world. They suggest that in my walking, I may even breathe in the pain of others and breathe out peace. I feel God working inside and outside of me to transform me by the simplest and most basic human function—my breathing, the life force within me, my life. I am learning so much about the God of my understanding from three diverse groups of friends— practicing Buddhists, practicing Christians, and members of 12-step groups. God speaks to us in so many mysterious ways if only we can stop and listen—and breathe it in.

Practice conscious breathing during your next morning or evening walk.

Psalm 85

**"Let me hear what God the LORD will speak,
for he will speak peace to his people,
to his faithful, to those who turn to him in their hearts."**

I am continuously amazed by the ways God works in my life. God constantly challenges me to live out my faith going in a different direction or with a new mindset, even when I think I am on the road of best intentions. This new direction most often comes in an interruption in my day, something not on my agenda.

My husband and I once served lunch every month at a city stewpot for the homeless in Little Rock. We were led there by a beautiful woman named Maggie who cooked at this kitchen almost daily. Maggie was herself on an extremely limited income and in poor health, but she still spent most of her life serving others. She brought a new direction to our lives. We met her by chance at a retreat and were never the same after that. I remember one Saturday we were late and were speeding down a major thoroughfare to the downtown church housing the inner-city meal. Suddenly an unshaven, dirty man with a garbage bag over his shoulder crossed the street in front of us. In my thoughts, I called out to him, "Get out of our way. We are late and are on the way to the stewpot!" Then my mind took a jolt. We had almost run over one we were hoping to serve! I came back to the present moment. I was reminded that God calls us to minister moment by moment. I may have a plan for good works, but God's timetable for the plan and my timetable may not be the same. I must stay open to the present moment and what God really wants me to do in that moment. This is very difficult for a closure person who lives by agendas.

With each unplanned interruption in your life today, stop and consider the possibility that this may be a message to turn to some new direction or allow more flexibility in your agenda. Be open to another plan besides your plan for this day.

Psalm 86

"Give ear, O LORD, to my prayer;
listen to my cry of supplication.
In the day of my trouble I call on you, for you will answer
me."

My husband and I once spent time at an exercise recommended by Keith Miller. We simply let each other speak without interruption for ten minutes about what was going on. Then the other repeated back what he had heard the other say without advice or judgment. We were practicing listening to each other and letting the other person know he had been heard. I am more and more convinced that ninety-nine percent of what people want in a relationship is to be heard. I wonder how often I do not listen to others, to my husband, to my children, to my partners, to my patients. I do not hear them because I am thinking about what I will say next or I do not listen because I am thinking about something else rather than concentrating on being present to them.

I have another friend who is severely hearing-impaired. She literally and figuratively does not listen to others. When she feels herself not being heard, or someone going against her or questioning her, her voice becomes louder and louder until she is almost screaming. Is she hoping that we will finally hear her or will be better listeners when she yells?

I long for God to hear me. Does God also long to be heard by us? Is this longing as great? My sense is that it is even greater, more than I can imagine.

Give a friend 10 minutes of listening time today and then tell your friend what you heard without making judgment or giving advice.

Psalm 87

"And of Zion it shall be said,
'This one and that one were born in it';
for the Most High himself will establish it.
The LORD records, as he registers the peoples,
This one was born there."

Visiting your childhood home where you were born and reared can be one of life's most bittersweet paradoxes — anticipation of a place that has stood still in your memory — realization that it has changed and you have changed — hope for healing of memories. I still well remember making that monumental trip just before my mother gave up our childhood home. I slept in my old bed for the last time and went through all my parent's possessions to choose which material memories I wanted to keep. I walked the streets I took to school, had one last visit by the river running by my home, rode a bicycle down "back street," and sat one last time in the choir stalls in the Methodist church where I was nurtured. I talked to an old girlfriend as if it had only been an hour since we last spoke. I saw a man who had been a star athlete and my idol when I was in high school. I still remember the number of his basketball jersey: forty-four.

Sometimes the nostalgia was too much and I had to break away. Indeed, I did come home early, partly because the experience was too intense. I talked to saints, everyday people who are angels unaware — most of whom I saw with new eyes on this last visit. I saw "ordinary people" who knew secrets I still haven't learned: a ninety-one-year-old neighbor who has battled a fractured hip and breast cancer and still walks every day to the drugstore at nine each morning to have a cup of coffee with a friend who formerly lived next door; another neighbor who cares for a ninety-three-year-old neighbor in a nursing home whose only relative, her sixty-year-old son, is a street person in New York; a next door neighbor with a heart of gold who cried when we left; a widower, a recovering alcoholic, whose life has been transformed by caring for animals and small children; the mother of a high school friend whose health is failing, who spends most of the year with her daughter out-of-state, but returns to her home at least a few weeks each year to "feel her roots;" a woman physician who gave her marriage and family a high priority and who has become one of the most nurturing physicians I know in an age where it has been more acceptable for women to be objective, focused, and masculine. For me she is a role model of a woman succeeding in her work using feminine values of relationship. I am still amazed by the serendipity that we met "by chance" at the post office on this last visit. I am constantly amazed by the way God works—throwing people in my path I need to see and learn from —if I will only see them or take time to talk to them.

I saw others who are models for a life I fear. I know how easily they got there—the pain of life on life's terms was too great to bear. My prayer for you and me today is that God will let us see when we are on that path, may we see the light in that darkness, and may our wounds be healed with God's tears: the alcoholic who only leaves her home once a week to go to the beauty parlor; the businesswoman who awakens at five in the morning each day so she won't have to dream and deal with her dreams; the couple whose only relationship in their marriage is convenience.

The miracle of life is the ordinary—the ordinary people in my small hometown who know everyone else's business but who also know what reaching out to others and caring is all about. The tragedy of life is also the ordinary—those who have retreated or escaped from life's everydayness because of the pain. Life is painful, sometimes unbearable. What turns us into survivors and lovers? Those in recovery would tell us that it is surrender to a power greater than ourselves and working the 12 steps. I've met people on this visit who have been doing this all their lives even though they may not have realized they have been part of a 12-step program.

God help me to be one too. [6]

Visualize ordinary people from your growing up years who are still role models for living. Be grateful and give thanks for their presence in your life.

Psalm 88

**"You rule the raging of the sea;
when its waves rise, you still them."**

She often swarms on me like an ocean wave. I sometimes do not know what has hit me. Sometimes there is an external storm, sometimes I have no idea what prompted this visit. The unwanted guest is depression, anger turned inward. I am powerless. Energy seems to evaporate from my mind and my body. I become like the Dead Sea, a body of water out of which nothing flows. My life turns inward and becomes stagnant. I feel dead inside, nothing will grow. I want this intruder to leave. I do not like her gifts. I tried to avoid or escape from her with drugs, alcohol, shopping, relationships, or food. This temporary relief eventually turned on me as well. Why me? How can I avoid this? The more I move out and share my pain, the more I see the unwanted guest as a circuit rider making frequent rest stops at many other watering holes.

The intruder is well known to many, maybe to most. Why does she visit? Is this the only way God can sometimes get my attention to slow down and change my life? I don't have answers. I only know that relief comes by getting professional medical help, riding the wave, looking further inward, seeing if there is some message, some wake-up call this visitor is announcing, and then trying to get up, walk out of the surf, get out of myself. The journey out does not need to be a lonely one. When I begin to surrender, seek help from others, ask for help from God and from my friends, especially those in recovery and professionals who are experienced in treating this common disease, work a 12-step program, look at character defects which may be blocking me from God , then I am usually on the way to healing. The visitor often seems to make her most frequent visits when my life centers on myself. I am beginning to think this may be a clue. The eventual calm that comes with the quieting of the wave is also real peace. It is the peace which passes understanding. If I can remember this, I will not be so devastated at her next visit.

Pray for peace for those you know who are riding the wave of anger turned inward—depression.

Psalm 89
"Remember, O LORD, how your servant is taunted; how I bear in my bosom the insults of the peoples."

I have a family member who is my shadow figure. Jungian psychologists would call her a part of my inner personality that I abhor in another person because I have not accepted that I inwardly have that trait in myself as well. She is the opposite of my image of myself. I often am repulsed by her presence. She is loud, self-centered, and lacking in common courtesy as well as basic table manners. The scary part is that as I age, I more and more gain awareness and begin to see the once well hidden parts of me that are like this person that are beginning to become more obvious. When she dies, who am I going to give those outrageously tacky Christmas gifts to that I love to buy? Whenever I have any question of who and what is my shadow, I go to visit or call this person. There is another woman at my church and in my recovery home group who is a similar shadow figure. She, too, is loud and sometimes insensitive. At times I think about not going to prayer or small group meetings when I think I might encounter her. One night some time ago, however, as we were praying together, I suddenly realized that my shadow was there praying evening prayers with me. The inner parts of me I could not accept were openly and physically there praying with me, beside me, and for me. What a wonderful image of my darker side—a side now well seen with more light.

Eastern traditions teach us to dialogue with our darker side and ask what it can teach us. My experience is that when I fail to do this, God puts actual persons in my life that simulate my shadow, which I must dialogue with openly for survival. What is even more amazing is that now, over the years, I am beginning to feel very differently about this "shadow" person. Through her rough edges I see a bright love that I actually am beginning to enjoy being around. I don't know whether my shadow figure has changed, but by some miracle of Grace, I am beginning to change. I am reminded of the saying on the wall in 12-step meeting rooms, "fake it until you make it." I also think of C.S. Lewis' quote about faith, "act as if," and it comes. I think these sayings meant to refer to our relationship to God can also relate to other people as well as hidden parts of ourselves we are not aware of. God has so many ways to teach us how to love him or her, ourselves, and others.

Do you have an image or a person who represents the parts of you which you cannot acknowledge or love? Imagine that person sitting or kneeling beside you at prayers.

Psalm 90
**"So teach us to count our days
that we may gain a wise heart."**

Our oldest son and I are traveling to Australia. We cross the international dateline just before we make a stop at Nadi on one of the Fiji Islands. I have an overwhelming sense of loss as we are told that we must move our watches ahead one whole day. One day is completely gone. I hope I will always remember August 4, 1995, for it was not a day in my life. I will try to talk to people who remember what they did on that Friday in late summer. I do hope I can remember a little of this feeling each day, remember how precious each day is, not spend the day regretting the past or obsessing about the trials of the future, try not to anticipate what will happen next, or agonize over whether the day will go according to my plan. I have a sense of the importance of living one day at a time. The significance of the next day, August 5, takes on even more importance. I have the privilege of being with my oldest son at the dawning of his twenty-fifth birthday. I will hold on to this moment and treasure this day as we fly halfway across the world together.

Pray that you may live in the precious present for this one day.

Psalm 91

"You will not fear the terror of the night,
or the arrow that flies by day ...
When they call to me, I will answer them;
I will be with them in trouble,
I will rescue them and honor them."

This Psalm was the favorite of a member of my first Education for Ministry (EFM) group, a program from an Episcopal seminary studying Hebrew and New Testament and church history and trying to apply it in our lives in ministry. She was not a regular church-goer. I vividly remember the first day of EFM how I smugly told myself that she was being hooked by God through this EFM group. I just knew by the time our four-year study was over, she would be a regular church attendee. That was almost twenty-five years ago. Our four-year program finished, but she continued in EFM for many more years. I think she still does not regularly attend an organized church, and I doubt if she realizes her favorite Psalm is usually read on St. Bartholomew's Day. She may have changed during the course; I know I did. I no longer have so much concern if she worships God in the same style as I do, or if she is "right" in her views about God. Her EFM group became her Christian community. My job is not to tell her how to worship, or to judge her worship, or to pray that she will worship a certain way. My job is to share with her in community the little glimpse of God I have known, to hear her stories of God, and to look for and glorify God shining through her — and God shines most beautifully in and through her.

Pray that we will not be blinded by our little knowledge of God. Pray that we will see how God is manifested in others in our community.

Psalm 92

"The righteous flourish like the palm tree,
and grow like a cedar in Lebanon.
They are planted in the house of the Lord;
they flourish in the courts of our God.
In old age they still produce fruit;
they are always green and full of sap."

Five members of my family have developed Alzheimer's. All have been God-loving saints who lived a life of caring and concern for others. I have seen brilliant minds turn into babble. Sometimes it is hard to remember what they were like before their mind left them. Our children especially have difficulty remembering what their grandparents were like when they were alive with energy and lust and curiosity for life. It is so hard to see beyond the shell that is left. It is impossible to understand how the end of life may be so cruel.

Of course, my greatest fear is that this will be my destiny as well. Last week I saw *Having Our Say*, the play about the remarkable Delaney sisters who lived to be over one hundred years old. I was given hope that life does not always end so tragically. This morning in my meditation I am given a flood of remembrances of how my family members used to be. I am overwhelmed by memories of their many unconditional kindnesses to me and others. I am reminded that the mind is not the ultimate. The heart is just as important in relationship. The heart is still there and always lingers long after the mind has faded. It is there for the asking, for the looking. When I next visit friends with Alzheimer's, I will not concentrate on what is not there, but on the heart which is still seen in some of the dullest of eyes. I have also learned this in recovery. A good life is not measured by our mind, our knowledge, how smart we are, but how we are in relationship to others, in relationship to God, ourselves, and each other.

Visit today with a loved one or friend whose mind has become disabled. Look and listen for her heart.

Psalm 93

"Your decrees are very sure;
holiness befits your house,
O LORD forevermore."

The most sacred part of the worship service of my tradition for me is when the congregation comes forward to receive communion. I try to pray for individuals as I see them coming to the altar. Sometimes I have a little knowledge of the wounds beneath the mask of calmness each of us wears. Sometimes I can feel or sense the tumult being carried to the high altar even by people I do not know. This is such a powerful and holy moment that often those "in control" masks we all wear will fade.

I especially love watching little children wait at the rail for a blessing and communion. Their little feet dance about on the beautiful needlepoint kneelers; their little heads are in every possible opening in the wood of the rail; and their little hands are in the most beautifully contorted opened positions. They look around to see if others are watching them. They have an expression of knowing they are doing something very special, out of the ordinary. I am always moved by that awesome look after they have tasted the wine. They know a mystery of the meal that grownups have forgotten.

One of my favorite movies is *Places In the Heart*. The conclusion of the movie is a communion service in a country Baptist church where the trays of grape juice and bread cubes are passed in the pews. Each person passes "the peace of God" as the Eucharistic elements are passed. All of the characters are dressed in their finest as they pass love and peace to each other. Living and dead characters in the story are there and pass communion and peace to those whom they previously in the movie attacked or even killed. It is truly a communion of saints passing the peace which passes all understanding. This has led me to imagine people at the rail who are absent or have never been there. I imagine my family, my friends, my coworkers, and I pray for them. Then I imagine those who have died also kneeling at the rail — loved ones and those with whom I still have unresolved relationships. Then I imagine my enemies — those with whom I have difficulty working or staying in relationship with. It is difficult to carry a resentment for someone as they kneel in silence even if it is in your imagination. This is the closest I come to seeing God within people with whom I have conflict and seeing them as unique gifts of God. I am often changed by the encounter.

Two people from the past have especially moved me at the altar — one in his stance and the other in his abstinence. I so well remember the visits to St. Mark's by a dearly loved "retired" priest in the diocese. He came usually with his daughter who was recovering from a stroke. She had difficulty kneeling, so she stood at the altar, and he stood up with her. This picture of the two of them stays with me as my image of how God stands by me in my humanness; when I am unable to kneel, God stands with me. Whatever position I am in, God is there in that same position even though I may not feel God's touch.

Another encounter at the altar occurred when our then-teenage son brought to church a Jewish friend who had spent the night with us. His friend obviously did not take communion, and John stayed back and sat with his friend while the rest of our family went to the altar. I saw and experienced a childlike sensitivity and sense of friendship that adult pride in our way often fails to bring to remembrance. Somehow his not taking communion at that moment seemed more Christ-like. Is it possible that we may sometimes commune best by sitting with those on the outside? I wish I could explain or understand this happening, but I know I learned a great lesson from my child about God's love. Perhaps someday I, too, will be able to show another God's love by sitting or standing when it is not the custom.

We are all observers of life at an altar rail in our homes, at our work, in nature, in our churches and mosques and synagogues, and at 12-step meetings. We witness a multitude bringing their burdens, known and unknown. What can we do to lighten each other's burden? For that moment all we can do is be there, but I have seen in my watch at the altar from at least two people that being there in relationship to each other is a powerful part of communion with God.

In your prayers, imagine those you love as well as those with whom you are carrying resentments for kneeling or standing or sitting before God and being embraced by that God love.

Psalm 94

"Understand, O dullest of the people;
fools, when will you be wise?
He who planted the ear, does he not hear?
He who formed the eye does he not see? ...
If the LORD had not been my help
my soul would soon have lived in the land of silence.
When I thought, 'My foot is slipping,'
your steadfast love, O LORD, held me up.
When the cares of my heart are many, your consolations
cheer my soul."

A friend returns from a retreat where the theme was "the demon of busyness." I should have gone with her, but of course I was too busy. I identified with all she said. Busyness is a demon that can devour your life. Filling my life with many tasks makes me feel important. My self-esteem is tied to my many busy accomplishments. Staying busy makes me feel significant, needed. When I am busy I do not have to deal with what is really going on in my life. When I become busy I am not open to God working in my life. I have an agenda which I must get through before I can do anything else. I am annoyed by people, even friends who get in my way. I hear another friend talk of starting out his day with a small list of tasks. On his way to one task, he thinks of several more he should do. He gets sidetracked and frustrated with all that he feels he should have done by the end of the day. He cannot rest because he is always adding things to do. I do the same thing. I walk into my kitchen to water my plants, and I see the dishwasher that needs emptying, and the mail that should be sorted, and an area that needs cleaning, and so on and so on. What is the answer? I do not know. I do know that God did not create us to perform endless tasks. We were created to love and serve God. I see a sign in a 12-step meeting room: "First

Things First." I long to learn something about priority, something about not needing closure for every task or idea, something about resting and waiting to know what the next right thing might be. I do know I always feel hope that my life will change after each meeting I attend. I also know that I have learned in recovery an awareness of my busyness. In the past, I thought it was just a natural and honored state. I am learning about a different life.

Pray that our ears and our eyes and our hearts will be opened, and we will become wise, and there will be healing from the busyness of this world.

Psalm 95

**"Let us come into his presence with thanksgiving;
let us make a joyful noise to him with songs of praise!"**

The first rule of St. Benedict tells us that our only hope is living a life in a spirit of thanksgiving. He encourages us to abandon attempts to achieve security or wealth. Only a life of gratitude for what we already have will bring peace. I met a woman this weekend living a life of thanksgiving. I was at my husband's high school reunion. She had lost her husband of thirty-five years a little over a year ago. She had lived through the first Christmas, the first summer, the first winter, the first autumn, the first spring without him. I had met her husband at the last reunion ten years earlier. She missed him terribly, but talked of gratitude for the life she had with him, a relationship few people know. She was waiting patiently and beginning to start a new life. Rarely have I seen such joy and thanksgiving for what a person had been given instead of anger for what had been taken away. It was something I wanted. I have seen it a few times in friends who have lost children. As their pain becomes more tolerable, they speak of gratitude for the time they had with their children. My prayer for today for you and for me is that we may begin to know that gratitude for friends, loved ones, and children while they are still with us as well as when we are apart.

I can not count the number of times I have talked to a spiritual friend about a difficulty, and her response has been to make a gratitude list of what is going right in my life. When I see two traditions such as 12-step recovery and the Benedictine Rule pointing to the same truth, it is a sign that this is indeed a real truth.

Gratitude is often an action that develops into a feeling. Peace comes most often when we become grateful for what

God has already given us instead of obsessing about what we don't have or have lost.

May our prayers today be of gratitude for the love we have been given through friends and family.

Psalm 96
"Sing to the LORD a new song."

O Lord, I want this day to be different. I want to sing a new song, dance a new dance. I want you to lead the dance, direct the song. I want to be a follower instead of the leader of the band. I sincerely no longer want to be the center of my world. I see and feel the pain and destruction that comes from trying to construct a universe that must accommodate my needs, my plans, my desires. I want to give up control to you. How do I do it? I have the desire, but I also have over 50 years of training in attempting to lead and manipulate others, including you, for my purpose. That was our relationship. I believed in you, because I needed you to accomplish my plan. God, I am ready for your plan. Mine has not worked. I have been blind to what I am. I have not seen the log in my own eye until I have encountered it in another. But now, by some painful miracle, a conflict with another controller like myself, I see in another a reflection of what I am and what I may become if I stay on this path. Help me. Mold me. Teach me how to love without asking for something back. Teach me how to be grateful for each moment, grateful for the many blessings of this life instead of regretting the tasks, the burdens I feel I have been given. Let me see them as stepping stones and not as stumbling blocks. Teach me about another way than my way. I want to sing a new song. I know I have no chance of doing it unless you take over and conduct me. I surrender this moment.

Just for today, join me in trying to sing a new song. Repeat "O Lord, I want this day to be different. I want to sing a new song, dance a new dance. I want you to lead the dance, direct the song. I want to be a follower instead of the leader of the band" at least three times throughout your day.

Psalm 97

"The LORD is king! Let the earth rejoice;
let the many coastlands be glad!
...His lightnings light up the world;
the earth sees and trembles.
...The heavens proclaim his righteousness."

Usually I look forward to Fridays, but when that Friday is the last day at the beach before returning home from vacation on the Gulf coast, I have intermittent periods of melancholy. That peace that comes with rest has been slow to come this week. Is it because I have been slow to rest? I have made frequent calls back to the hospital to check on things. I have spent too much time cooking—something I love doing on vacation because I am too tired to do it at the end of the day at home. But balance and moderation are deaf words to my ears. I must do a job to excess.

Tranquility has come, however, and now on the last day, for almost one whole day, I have enjoyed each precious moment as a gift. I have felt the wind—warm, cool, wet, and dry. I have sat on our balcony and watched the ever-changing blue sea in all its splendor. I have felt a little of the salty taste of *being* rather than *doing*—what Joseph Campbell calls "the experience, the rapture of being alive." I have ridden the waves, sat in awe of a spectacular pink and blue sunrise and sunset, watched the birds hunt for food and the dolphins play, and have been warmed by the sun, the wind, and a gentle summer rain. I have noticed the subtle changes of constancy of life in my surroundings. I have thrilled in the experience of living that moment instead of feeling guilty about the past or anxious about the future. Today the promises have come true: *I have known a new freedom and a new happiness. I have comprehended the word serenity. I have realized that God is doing for me what I could not do for myself.*[7]

Yet I contemplate on how long the peace will last and will I take some of this serenity back home with me.

Why has it taken me so long to realize that the peace of God, the presence of something greater than myself, is so apparent in the natural spectacle of the world around me — the earth and sea — but I do not have time or eyes to see it. And now again in a few hours we will leave. Will I take home with me the rhythm of the waves, the most tranquil sound I know — the constant reminder of the continuity of life and time? Will I take time to see the wind, other birds, other sunsets when I am back at my home and work? When I return home will I become too busy to observe the beauty that awaits me from that balcony of my routine life? God, I know — no, I feel — you will be with me next Friday — but will I still see and feel you as I do today? [8]

Spend as much time as possible this day outside experiencing the present moment in your natural surroundings. This is where so many can see and feel most clearly the presence of God, something greater than ourselves.

.

Psalm 98

"Let the sea roar, and all that fills it;
the world and those who live in it.
Let the floods clap their hands;
let the hills sing together for joy at the presence of the Lord."

I am remembering a visit to Monterey Bay, where the sea literally roars with the sound of the waves and the California sea lions. We visit a local church, St. Mary's By-the-Sea in nearby Pacific Grove. There is a striking stained glass window above the altar of the annunciation. Mary is listening to the angel as she reads by the sea. Was Mary really sitting by the sea when she was told of the new life that was to come to her? The colorful but simple window is meaningful to me because I know I often think I am closest to the voice of God by the sea or ocean. It may be the rhythm of the roaring waves, which is often the only sound that can drown out and silence the committee that constantly speaks in my head. It may be the overwhelming beauty of the water life—the flock of pelicans gracefully flying in a regimented line close to the sea, the tall blue heron stalking the water's edge, the scurrying sand pipers, the rushing crabs, the multicolored starfish, the barking sea lions, the sleek paired dolphins, the sea otters on their backs with their meals on their tummies. When I am at the ocean, I take time to feel the wind, get up for the sunrise, stop for the sunset, and wait and watch for the moon rise. I become aware that there is a power much greater than myself who created beauty beyond comprehension. I begin to know and begin to live the gratitude for our creator and our lives which is expressed no more beautifully than in these last Psalms.

Today sit or imagine yourself by a body of water. Put the beauty of the natural world around you at the top of your gratitude list.

Psalm 99
"O LORD our God, you answered them;
You were a forgiving God to them."

I still grieve my mother's recent death. My mother and I had a difficult relationship. I had no idea her death would be so hard. This experience is teaching me that some of the greatest grief when a loved one dies occurs when there is still estrangement in the relationship. Issues were not resolved. I keep thinking about my part in this estrangement with my mother. I never completely made amends to her for my part. Now I wish I had. I did not make it home to see my mother before she died. Perhaps this is another part of my grief and my guilt. I grieve for the relationship that we will now never have. Each time I would go home, I had expectations that things would be different. Now this will never be a reality. I did not use the wisdom of the Serenity Prayer in my relationship with my mother. I kept hoping she would change when my only hope was changing myself and how I reacted to her.

There is also now a realization of loneliness when both parents are dead that I never expected. Healing comes as I try to reach out of myself and my feelings of guilt and inadequacy. I will never become the image of the daughter I wanted to be to my parents. I wish I could have taken my mother communion in the hospital before she died. This Sunday shortly after arriving home from my mother's funeral, a friend called me to bring communion to her mother who had just miraculously recovered from a life-threatening illness. As I stood at the bedside, I realized a striking resemblance of my friend's mother to my own. Amazing how God allows us to heal by leading us to do for someone else what we are not capable of doing for my own loved ones. God's ways are mysterious and wonderful. I reach out to others with selfish

166

motives. God continues to comfort me and use me even with all my defects.

Pray for forgiveness and healing of your own family relationships. Make amends if possible.

Psalm 100

"Make a joyful noise to the LORD, all the earth.
...Enter his gates with thanksgiving, and his courts with praise.
Give thanks to him, bless his name.
For the LORD is good;
His steadfast love endures forever,
And his faithfulness to all generations."

We meet our granddaughter, Langley, in Washington, D.C. for her eighth birthday. It is her first trip to Washington. I am at the National Cathedral for a conference and my husband comes along to be a tour guide for our granddaughter while I am at the meeting. We talk about all the sites to show her, the Washington Monument, the Smithsonian, the White House, National Archives, and of course worshiping at the National Cathedral. I think of all the courts of praise, the many cathedral chapels I want to show her: the Children's Chapel, the Bethlehem Chapel and my favorite, the Chapel of the Good Shepherd. We walk through this magnificent gothic cathedral. What will she most want to see? Of course it is the Children's Chapel. She is also engaged by the outside areas surrounding the cathedral, places I never spent a great deal of time during the many visits we have made to the cathedral. She loves the intricate paths through the Bishop's garden. There with her I am drawn to the statue of the prodigal son where it is difficult to tell whether the son is male or female and if God is male or female. Her favorite place at the National Cathedral, however, is a little garden secretly tucked away in the middle of the Cathedral College. It is surrounded by the walls of the Cathedral College, previously called the College of Preachers. There is an apricot tree, a fountain, cardinals, and a bird's nest whose owner we never identify. We spend hours there while she dances and "makes a joyful noise" on the brown grass. We also picnic on the grounds between the Cathedral College and Langley makes friends with the brown and black squirrels and the cardinals and robins and calls them each by a name she has given them. True to form, children teach us a world we once knew and thrived in and have forgotten or ignored.

Langley has one disappointment that we know of on the trip. For years she identified Washington as the home of the ruby red slippers that Judy Garland as Dorothy wore in the *Wizard of Oz* and are now displayed in the Museum of American History. Langley has been an *Oz* fan I think since birth. My husband takes her to the exhibit, and disappointingly they hear it is closed. Langley immediately accepts it and says, "Let's go on to the Air and Space Museum. We will see the ruby slippers on our next trip." Acceptance. Another gift we can also learn from children of another generation. Another day goes by where God shows us so much beauty, strength, and hope through someone else's eyes as our vision has been clouded by the world view: the eyes of an eight-year-old.

Spend time today with some of your favorite children and learn from them about acceptance of situations out of their control as well as beauty in the world outside that we fail to see as we wear our grownup glasses.

Psalm 101

"One who secretly slanders a neighbor
I will destroy.
A haughty look and an arrogant heart
I will not tolerate."

I have worked often with someone who constantly puts other people down, looking for and pointing out mistakes others have made. I secretly call him "the hall monitor." He seems to be able to find his own self-worth by criticizing and revealing the faults of others. This seems to be a mechanism of survival for him. For years I have tried many maneuvers to change him. I tried countering his attacks by looking for his mistakes and quickly pointing them out. But then I became like him, and I did not enjoy being the world's critic.

I tried beating myself up for the errors he pointed out and sought to be as perfect as possible. But alas, I soon erred again. It is not only my condition but the human condition. I have tried to be hypercritical of myself. If I can point out my mistakes before others do, it is more acceptable. But alas, soon my "friend" finds some defect of which I had no awareness. The Serenity Prayer tells me that I will not be able to change this other person's behavior. My only hope for relationship is to change the way I react to him. I can realize his method and try not to take it personally. I can try not to be devastated by the mistakes he points out and learn from them. I can try to let him know how I feel when he is so critical. I can try not to play into his pathology. I am working on progress, not perfection. The most helpful part of this relationship has been a glimmer of awareness of that same critic also secretly living inside of me and devouring others and me. It is a natural inhabitant of all of us, but seems to have a more prominent place at the table in some. The critic, like all our character defects, is so often difficult to see in ourselves, but is glaringly present in others. I am beginning to recognize her inner voice. I am asking her to spend some time with the compassionate part of me. What a wonderful marriage, awareness with compassion. We must become aware of our mistakes, our defects, but when we can accept our humanness with love, the result may be so different. We must examine with compassion our own errors and those of others. We must examine our part in our defects, talk about the mistakes to another person and God, surrender the defect in prayer to God, and make amends to others for the harm we have done when possible. Otherwise the critic living alone inside of us will not be well tolerated and will destroy us and others. Living with awareness with compassion for ourselves and others is like being on a very different path. It is journeying on a road less traveled.

Become aware of the critical part of you who secretly slanders a neighbor. Pray that it will become aware of the compassionate part of you and that they can work and live together.

Psalm 102

"Hear my prayer, O LORD;
let my cry come to you.
Do not hide your face from me
in the day of my distress.
Incline your ear to me;
answer me speedily in the day when I call."

    A crisis occurred in my medical group while I was out of town. I spent a great deal of time on the phone and many hours when I returned working on a solution. I had to leave town again. I constantly prayed for guidance about the problem and prayed individually for my partners almost hourly while I was gone. When I returned home I immediately called one of my partners to plan strategy for our next move. To my astonishment, I found out my partners had solved the dilemma without me! One partner in particular had stepped forward and addressed the issue. Instead of being relieved, I was disappointed. I had wanted God to allow me to be the leader in bringing resolution to this issue. I wanted to be the winning warrior in this battle. Instead, God had chosen someone else. I am learning a little about God's answer to prayer. I am learning that I am not God, not in charge of the universe with all the answers. I pray that I may stay open to God's answer to prayer.

Pray without ceasing and be open to God's answer. It will come, but often not in the envelope or even sent by the messenger you expected.

Psalm 103

"Bless the LORD, O my soul,
and do not forget all his benefits--
who forgives all your iniquity,
who heals all your disease, who redeems your life from the
Pit,
who crowns you with steadfast love and mercy,
who satisfies you with good as long as you live
so that your youth is renewed like the eagle's...
He does not deal with us according to our sins,
nor repay us according to our iniquities."

Who is God? What is God like? What are the attributes of the God of my understanding? If we are made in God's image, what does God want us to be like? What have the Psalms taught us about the qualities of God? God is not a controlling God. God creates. God listens. God comforts. God rejoices with us. God weeps with us. God protects us. God takes great pleasure in us. This Psalm tells us specifically that God heals us, redeems us, shows us love and mercy, loves us beyond our comprehension, satisfies us, renews us, and forgives us. I think I most often forget this last quality of God. God's great image is to forgive. The Bible and the Psalms constantly relate to us stories of God's forgiveness. The more I can forgive another, the more chance I have of being closer to God. I find this to be a highly motivating reason to pray that I can forgive others who have harmed me. It also motivates me to pray that I will be forgiven for the harm I have caused to myself and to others. It constantly calls me to work steps 4-9, becoming aware of the wrongs I have done to others, letting one other person and God know about, surrendering to God, asking to be changed, and making amends to that person if possible. When I can forgive, I am freed from that terrible bondage that a resentment brings as it consumes my life. I am no longer a victim but a participant in God's creation. My life does not center around how I have been harmed but rejoices in the God of my understanding who loves me by creating my life for his or her pleasure.

Pray for the ability to forgive others and yourself and be freed of resentment. Pray for the freedom that comes with forgiveness.

Psalm 104

**"You set a boundary that they may not pass,
so that they might not again cover the earth."**

I seek out my spiritual friend about a person I have to work with on a regular basis whose words and actions are verbally hurtful. Each time I am with the person, a mound of resentments builds up with each encounter. I tire of these interactions and having to spend so much of my energy working through these resentments. My spiritual friend suggests that I must forgive with boundaries. If I do not set up boundaries with the person who keeps wounding me, I will continue to be hurt time after time. This is what people in recovery call insanity: doing the same thing over and over again and expecting a different result. How do I change? Boundaries were not part of my upbringing. It is a new word in my vocabulary. She tells me to see if I have some part in his hurtful behavior, make amends if it fits, and then forgive. But if I encounter that person and his wounding behavior again, I must let him know I am hurt by these words and actions on his part and may have to distance myself from the relationship. I also must go into the relationship without expectations that this person will change, but I am trying to change the way I react to him. I must let him know how I feel when I hear his verbal unkindnesses. My survival depends not on changing this person but on changing my reaction to his behavior. When I am in conflict with another person, my job is to gather information and articulate as clearly as possible how I feel about the situation. Then I must turn the results over to God. Sometimes the pain of being in relationship to this person is too great, and I must place a real or imaginary distance between us until I feel safer. Sometimes I imagine an invisible glass shield around me when I encounter someone who seems constantly to wound me. I must have no expectations of this person. I also ask friends in recovery to pray for me when I must encounter this person. The greatest healer is for me to offer daily prayer for this person. Before I am healed, I may ultimately have to keep even tighter boundaries between us if the wounding continues. I hope to gain knowledge by observing friends in recovery who are much better than I am at boundary setting.

Today observe someone in your life who is good at boundary setting. Consider reading about boundaries. There are many good books; one is **Breaking Free** *by Pia Mellody and Andrea Wells Miller.*

Psalm 105

**"Remember the wonderful works he has done,
his miracles."**

It is a cold windy day at the beach. The tall tan and green sea oats bend their heads towards the ocean. The wind blows in from the north, driving the waves out to sea so that the turquoise ocean is almost still. No waves hit the shore. A lone fishing boat slowly motors by very near the shore. At the horizon I can barely make out a barge in the distance. An orange and black Monarch butterfly floats by. It may be conserving energy for its unbelievably treacherous flight from the Alabama gulf coast to a valley in central Mexico. I stop for a brief second to say a prayer that it will make it. A single osprey flies majestically high overhead, making carefully calculated crashing dives to the sea in search of its breakfast. The intensely bright sunlight shines directly on the water in front of me. The shimmering of the wind on the waves gives the ocean a constant appearance of tiny sparkling lights rising and falling out from the sea. A flock of pelicans float and dive amidst the bright twinkling spectacle. Pairs of dolphins intermittently swim and arch in and out of my field of view. Five Blue Angels soar by in formation overhead as if they are saluting the spectacle below them. As I look out from my balcony I see very few people walking on the beach. It is too cold and windy for southerners. Alas, a man wearing a wind breaker, gloves, and stocking hat walks out onto the white sand and goes to the surf, but instead of observing the ocean turned into a blanket of shining stars, he pulls out his cell phone and starts talking with his back to the sea. He is missing a once-in-a-lifetime scene. But soon my inner critic reminds me that I have been acting very similarly. Before coming to the balcony, I had spent my morning at a local deli with wifi to check my email. I as well have trouble staying disconnected —

disconnecting from the frantic busyness of agendas and tasks to be accomplished and instead reconnecting with the everyday beauty and vastness of a power greater than ourselves.

Put your agendas and work down for five minutes. Go outside and connect to the natural beauty of your world made by a power greater than yourself. Give thanks for this creation.

Psalm 106

**"But they soon forgot his works;
they did not wait for his counsel."**

I am absolutely certain I know how to solve an issue this week at work. I know I have come up with the right answer to this problem. The facts and the solution seem very clear. I seek very little counsel from others in making my decision about the matter. The solution is obvious. I am a very strong closure person (J or judgmental on Meyers-Briggs personality indicator). If there is a problem, I want it fixed and as soon as possible. In my haste towards solution, I am beginning to realize that I often overlook or do not even consider possibilities that may be much better than my own. As I present my solution to this problem to those involved, it becomes clear I have not evaluated the problem as thoroughly as I should have. I have been too certain of the answer from the start. I begin to have some realization that I may not know all the answers. I may not be as smart as I thought. The solution would have been so much better if I had sought counsel from several others and investigated more facts before coming to closure. I do not know what is best for the world, or even my family, or even myself. Then in my awareness, I feel tremendous relief rather than disappointment in my limited knowledge. It is absolutely freeing no longer to feel you must be in charge of the universe. It is the new freedom that is offered in the promises.

Pray that you will take time in making decisions to ask for guidance from God often through the many friends God has provided around you. Pray that you will be enabled to wait for guidance rather than rushing into solutions.

Psalm 107

**"He sent out his word and healed them,
and delivered them from destruction."**

Tonight I attend a healing service at my local church. As members kneel for healing, many members of the congregation come up to lay on hands with their priest. There is a community praying and reaching out to one another for healing. Couples kneel together; mothers and daughters, fathers and sons, kneel together. Members who cannot kneel because of handicaps stand while members of the community reach out to them. Obviously ill members kneel and ask for healing for other members of their family or friends.

I am especially moved by a small child who asks an older woman as she leaves the altar, "When he laid his hand on you, did it hurt?" Children ask the most wonderful questions. Yes, my experience is that healing hurts. Anyone who has had surgery or any physical injury knows well the many painful days, sometimes weeks and months, that accompanies healing. It is often a very slow process as well. My experience is that spiritual healing is the same. Healing is made bearable by the kind of people I worshipped with tonight. My experience is that I must first realize my woundedness and ask for healing. I must be on my knees. Something mystical occurs in God's healing which I cannot explain. Even all my years of medical practice do not offer any hope of explanation, only more mystery. I do know that God's healing has best been experienced by me in community. The Holy Spirit, God, often best reaches me through the voice, the touch, the talent, the labor, the love of others. I have experienced much physical and spiritual healing in my life, and I experience it again tonight.

Consider attending a healing service at your place of worship if it is part of your tradition.

Psalm 108
**"Be exalted, O God, above the heavens,
and let your glory be over all the earth."**

Our oldest son and I decided to go on a mother-son trip to the beach together when he was in high school. It was an adventure for both of us, for neither of us had driven the nine hour journey by ourselves. It was our first trip for just the two of us together without the rest of our family. I have pleasant memories of the week together, but what I remember the most is the morning we left. Early that morning, I went to the balcony of our condo to return towels to the storeroom. Down the beach it was raining and up the beach the sun was shining, and there in front of our balcony was a rainbow. It ended in front of our condominium. Little fishing boats were going in and out of the rainbow's end. I was at the end of the rainbow. I was experiencing a once-in-a-lifetime event. And yet I said, "How nice," and went to put up the towels. When I returned in a few seconds, the rainbow was gone. Today I keep thinking, how many rainbows have I missed because I was putting up towels?

On our way home as we approached Memphis, I saw a double rainbow—another spectacle I had never seen. When we returned home we learned that Maggie Herndon, a dear friend who had led us to the stewpot ministry, had unexpectedly died that day. In my compulsive need to find meaning, I wondered if the rainbows had been the heavens rejoicing for the life of a beautiful saint.

Most of my life is centered around myself as "God," my comprehensive agenda, and my plan for the rest of the day and the rest of my life. I sometimes have faint glimpses of the true love and presence of God in others and in myself; but when I am outdoors, especially at the beach, something remarkable happens, if I am open to it. I begin to smell and taste and see God and God's unbelievable plan, which is too large for me to comprehend. God is there every day in my every waking moment, but I am usually too busy *doing* to see the *being*.

The glory of God in all the earth and the heavens above is always there. It is there to bring me out of my gloom. It is there to show me how loved I am. It is there to bring me out of myself and my self-centered state and my very structured agenda. It is there to lead me to the knowledge of something: a world, and beyond, greater than myself. It is there for the asking, if I can only stop and see and feel and smell and hear it.

Today spend time looking to the heavens, to the clouds, for an awareness of the presence of God in this world and in your life.

Psalm 109

"Do not be silent, O God of my praise,
For wicked and deceitful mouths are opened against me,
speaking against me with lying tongues.
They beset me with words of hate,
and attack me without cause."

I am the object of a barrage of criticism in my work. Some of the criticism I need to hear, some is not justified. A visit from the critic is never pleasant. I have lived a life of trying to be good enough so I would not be the object of criticism. This is not the human condition. I am slowly learning that critical remarks can be very helpful. I should listen to them, discuss them with someone else, especially a spiritual friend or a friend in recovery and see if there is something there for me to change or correct. Of course criticism is always easier to swallow when it comes from a loving friend. I am fortunate to have such a friend who can tell me when I am off track. I am not offended by her remarks because I realize she loves me as unconditionally as possible. There is nothing in it for her when she talks to me. This is the role of a spiritual friend or counselor.

What do we learn when we are unjustly criticized or attacked? This, too, is the human condition. It will happen to all of us and we will also do it to someone else. My recent experience has taught me the pain of being wrongly accused. This morning I am at another meeting where someone else is wrongly criticized. The feeling of criticism that is not merited is acutely with me. For the first time that I can remember, I speak up for that person and against the accusations. I had never done that before, for there was no advantage or gain for me in doing so. This time I had walked in those shoes. I know the pain and humiliation she is feeling. A little of my world stops centering on me and reaches out, ever so briefly, to another for little visible gain.

Today consider speaking out for an injustice done to someone else. It will change your life.

Psalm 110
"From the womb of the morning,
like dew, your youth will come to you."

This morning I find an old diary that I kept over fifty years ago when I was eleven, twelve, and thirteen. I have not been able to put down the worn green book with the secret gold lock. The writing is mostly factual, not very personal, but still I am amazed with what was going on in my life at that time. I spent my days being taken to music lessons by my mother, playing or performing music, visiting my grandparents, studying, and going to church with my mother and my grandparents. Now a half a century later, I see that my life is not much different. My grandparents and my mother have been dead for some time, but otherwise, my life is very similar. I am impressed with the many performances that were central to my life: talent shows, my grandmother's circle meetings, PTA meetings, school concerts, school plays, church events, picnics. I do not remember any of them, but I can still feel the pain and feeling of failure when I wrote about the times I did not do well. This need to perform is still such a part of me. I did not realize it was so embedded in my early youth. Was this the way I learned to feel good—or bad—about myself?

After sixty years I have little glimpses of God's love in my life: a love which does not require a performer, a love that is given to me because the God of my understanding loves me as her child, a love greater than I can imagine or feel, a love which guides and directs my day when I will allow it. I also know that God uses me even in my defects: my need to perform to gain approval and love of others. I know that some of the music I make, some of my sermons, may have touched the soul of someone else, even though my motive sometimes may have been for recognition rather than reaching out. I also know that one of the safest and most comfortable spaces is still in community. This was true as a child, and it is still true as an adult. Worshipping with a community of believers, reading the liturgy, preaching, playing the harp, singing with friends, hearing the word, serving at the altar, receiving communion is still a mainstay of my life. This is where I learn to get back on track as I often stray. This is also where I consistently am reminded of this love which never dies and will sustain me through the joy and trials of this life. It is a place where I learn to reach out beyond my own selfish motives. I give thanks to parents and grandparents who led me into this way of life by their example.

My mother and I struggled with our relationship for many years. Today I realize that my relationship with God began because of the exposure she gave me as a child to the church where the God of my understanding was a loving and caring God. I give thanks for all the music lessons she drove me to, which led to my great love for this universal language. I also give thanks for the founders of 12-step recovery who before I was born birthed a program that would save my life, a program that had at its core a belief in this same God. I realize I needed one more community to teach me to surrender to God.

Find some writing you made as a child. Give thanks for those who were so important to you in those growing up years and made sacrifices for you which you may have forgotten today.

Psalm 111

"Praise the LORD!
I will give thanks to the LORD with my whole heart,
in the company of the upright, in the congregation.
Great are the works of the LORD,
studied by all who delight in them."

I rest and read today. It is one of those beautiful rainy days where watching and hearing the wind and the waves from my window brings calm and peace. I intermittently go out and feel the mist and the wind. Then I am called back to some task. As I become obsessed with my agenda, I find it hard to stop. I am slowly seeing glimpses of how I may be healed or at least relieved of my need for busyness. I know when I become so engrossed in my work, I have great difficulty stopping to rest and re-center. I often continue until I am physically and mentally exhausted. Then I seek out some addiction to bring me relief so that I may start the process all over again. For many years I have been drawn to monastic rules of life. I have been especially drawn to the Benedictine Rule through several recent writings: *The Cloister Walk* by Kathleen Norris, *Always We Begin Again* by John McQuiston, and writings by Ester de Waal. I am learning that I must each day stop, pray, offer thanksgiving, study, or reflect, or I will have very little peace. I will not be called to my addictions for relief from my pain. I know that I must have these times systematically scheduled in my day. Otherwise, I will not stop; I am too busy. These times are no longer an option, they are a necessity. Experience has shown me that I get more accomplished if I make these attempts to re-center, open my heart to what God may really want me to do this day. For me a rule of life has become a roadmap to healing. It has been an answer to prayer. I can individually keep little bits of my rule. I have more success in community. More and more I realize that meeting in community, once a week, once a day, is just as important as my solitary encounter with the God of my understanding. More and more in community I hear the still, small voice that is often deadened by the community in my mind.

Develop a rule of life. Consider practicing part of your rule with the help of some type of community or congregation.

Psalm 112

"It is well with those who deal generously and lend,
who conduct their affairs with justice.
For the righteous will never be moved;
They will be remembered forever."

As I write, my husband and one of our sons are in New York City, doing the town before Christmas. I think about several years ago when we took our oldest son to New York when he was a senior in high school. We were awed that he enjoyed having room service for dinner as much as seeing the sites of the Big Apple. I will always remember another incident with our son as we walked the streets of the big city. This was the first time he had encountered people begging on the streets. In our worldly sophistication my husband and I were hardened to their presence and quickly walked by and ignored the unkempt men and women with handwritten signs sitting on curbs or between tall skyscrapers. Our son could not. We walked down two blocks, and finally as we were walking the third block, he stopped, turned around and went back to give money to a young man we had earlier passed. I was overcome with his compassion. I was overcome by his ability to reach out in a strange and new situation when his parents had not set the example. He dared to take action when all around him where acting differently. I know we cannot feed all the hungry we see each day, but neither should they be ignored, treated as faceless members of our community. My prayer is that I will always remember my son's compassion. May I still keep and hold onto that compassionate desire and longing to reach out to those in need that only a child knows before he is overcome and hardened by all the neediness of the cold world. May I never again take suffering as the norm. May I retain at least a glimmer of the world view through the compassionate eyes of a child observing suffering for the first time. I am reminded of three of the promises of 12-step recovery:

- We will lose interest in selfish things and gain interest in our fellows.
- Self-seeking will slip away.
- Our whole attitude and outlook upon life will change.[9]

That day I was taught what these promises mean by a young teenager.

Mediate on how these three promises can come true in your life.

Psalm 113

"He gives the barren woman a home,
Making her the joyous mother of children.
Praise the LORD."

I so well remember the day my husband retired from his medical practice and his patients returned to say thank you and good-bye. His primary work had been operating on children with cleft palates and lips, restoring these children to a life of beauty and hope. It was so moving to see the gratitude of these children and their parents for his work. I treasure the picture of him with these patients at his retirement. I knew this was an experience that I would only know secondhand, through him, for my medical specialty is pediatric radiology. Most of the patients I help never know or see me or the work I have done to help restore them to health. It is the downside of being in a medical specialty where you deal more with other physicians than with patients. However, I had a monumental experience recently when as I attended the twenty-fifth birthday of the neonatal unit at Arkansas Children's Hospital. I had been at Children's when the neonatal intensive care unit was born. Patients and their parents who had been cared for in this intensive care unit returned to celebrate this great anniversary. I was in a room filled with children most of whose X-rays I had read, on whom I had performed many procedures. Some I knew I had helped care for and diagnose their condition. The children and their parents would not know me, and I would never know them. Most of my prayers for them had been in secret, as I learned to know their inner being only in the black and white of their X-rays. But there was an overwhelming feeling of being in a room full of people whom I had known intimately and had in some small way walked beside on a journey in the first days of their lives. Perhaps sometimes I helped them, restored them to life or given them a new life. We would never know each other. I knew life had some meaning as I saw these children, many now adults. I cried with joy. I thought of so many other hidden employees of this hospital who have made a difference in lives by simply doing the job they were given: housekeepers, pharmacists, operating room nurses, and helicopter pilots that these families would never know. I knew God had used all of us for a purpose, often when we had forgotten about it or were unaware. It did not matter that we did not recognize each other. We had a beautiful secret bond of helping each other on this journey and I felt so grateful that we had secretly known each other.[10]

Give thanks today for people that may be unknown to you that have made a difference in your life.

Psalm 114

**"Tremble, O earth, at the presence of the LORD,
at the presence of the God of Jacob."**

I still so well remember the day I visited the room of an eight-year-old girl dying of cancer at Children's Hospital. I went to perform a test to try to explain and relieve some of her suffering. Her disease and its treatment had greatly disfigured her body. Her head was almost bald with sparsely scattered streaks of once curly blonde hair. The dark sunken eyes on her ashen face were highlighted by purple blotches beneath her pale skin from previous bleeding episodes. Her paper-thin skin seemed attached directly to the bones of her arms and legs. Her breathing was intermittent and labored. Each movement of her frail body took all of her energy. She was in constant pain. As I entered her room, I was overcome immediately by her suffering — so unjust, unfair, unreasonable. This has been my closest experience of the horror of the crucifixion. But in the midst of this great suffering I also encountered something even more overpowering. This young innocent had not been abandoned. She was not alone. Lying in bed beside the almost lifeless child was her grandmother. I remember the grandmother's unkempt black hair, the rough skin of her large flabby arms, and her flowered print dress showing just above the covers. What I remember the most, however, is that this grandmother's huge body was embracing and surrounding this precious inhuman suffering. I stood in awe, for I knew I was on holy ground. I was in the presence of the living God. I will never forget the great, gentle arms and body of this grandmother. She never spoke while I was there. She was holding and participating in suffering that she could not relieve, and somehow her *silent* presence was relieving it. No words could express the magnitude of her love. I had been there before. I knew immediately that this was what my grandmother would have done for me if I had been that child. I performed my test as quickly as possible, but stood at the door a moment longer, the image of this little girl and her grandmother searing into my heart. In silence I turned and walked out, the door shutting gently behind me. [11]

Pray for an awareness of the magnitude of God's presence and love in your life especially if you are in the midst of suffering. You may be walking on holy ground.

Psalm 115

"They have mouths, but do not speak;
Eyes, but do not see.
They have ears, but do not hear;
noses, but do not smell.
They have hands, but do not feel;
Feet, but do not walk;
They make no sound in their throats."

I regularly phone a relative who almost never expresses any interest in what is going on in the life of our own family. As soon as she picks up the phone, she starts talking about what has been happening to her. I long for her to show some sign that she is interested in what we are doing. She may be interested, but she does not express it. Each time I call, I think it will be different. It never is. This is insanity on my part—doing the same thing over and over and expecting different results. This person may never change. She hasn't in nearly seventy years. My only hope of finding peace is for me to change. One option is just not to call her, isolate from her. I have tried that, but there is still something pulling me to be connected to her. I feel a commitment to the relationship. I don't know what this is. I do know what I can do, and that is to change my expectations of her. Maybe she has only a few friends to whom she can tell her story. She may be very lonely. Maybe this is the gift I have to offer her, a listening ear. Now when I call, I try not to expect her to ask about our lives. When I rationally think about it, it seems ridiculous that I require everyone I talk to to be interested in me. Am I that needy? I have so many other friends with whom I can share myself. I pray that my relationship with this person will change and that I will not keep asking this person to offer something she cannot give.

Pray today for yourself and another person with whom you are having difficulty. Pray that you can accept her and love her where she is.

Psalm 116

"For you have delivered my soul from death,
my eyes from tears,
my feet from stumbling.
I walk before the Lord in the land of the living.
I kept my faith, even when I said, 'I am greatly afflicted.' "

I am having a flare-up of arthritis. I have been pain-free for years, and suddenly it returns like an ugly monster, literally grounding me. I cannot take my daily walks. I must wear a brace for pain relief. I must dramatically slow down the pace of my life. I go to work and only a few of my co-workers ask me how I feel or inquire if they can help me. I feel more and more a victim of life's misery, and no one cares. Self-pity consumes me like a thundering wave and I am hopelessly drowning in my physical and mental pain. I talk to a spiritual friend. I pour out to her my misery and the pain and loneliness I feel. She listens to me and repeats back to me what I have said to her. She is an active listener. She does not tell me what to do, but I immediately know what I must do for relief as I hear my words outside of my head. I let some of my partners know my pain. They did not know. I, of course, had expected them to read my mind and body language. They also let me know where they are. They are also in some physical or mental pain. I understand now where they are and why they could not reach out to me. I also can step back and see that in my pain I found myself at the center of the universe, expecting all to respond to my hurt. Now I have a little insight that I may not be the only one suffering. I give thanks for my spiritual friend who called and reached out to me, who listened to me, who never told me what to do, but in her listening caused me to remember the next right step — communication. Also, as I heard someone else's story, my own story lost some of its power over me. My own burden became lighter as I heard the burden of someone else and sat and walked beside them.

Ask one other person today how they are truly doing and listen to what they say. Don't try to fix them, just listen and sit or walk with them.

Psalm 117

**"For great is his steadfast love toward us,
and the faithfulness of the LORD
endures forever."**

I am constantly amazed by the faithfulness of God. While my many character defects block my relationship with God, God seems still to be there, waiting patiently, longing for relationship, giving more than I can comprehend, caring for me and those whom I have neglected and forgotten to wait for or be faithful to.

I think of times in my life when God has waited for me. I immediately think of our children. I was so involved in my career and my addictive lifestyle during their early growing up years. When I realized all the time I had missed with them, some were almost grown. Was it too late for relationship? Had I missed the most important years? I had not been there for so many things with them. After our two oldest children finished college, they both returned home for several years. Many friends talked about this with horror, but I saw it through the Grace of God in a new light. God had given me another chance to find relationship with my children at a different age in a new way.

It seems we have so many opportunities for redemption. We make wrong choices, but God constantly gives us new opportunities. God waits for us until we are ready to do the job we have been given, and then gives us another chance in a new situation, usually not one we had planned.

I think of my relationship with my religious tradition. I was very involved as a child, but stopped attending religious services in college. I didn't need them. I infrequently returned to the church at times of crises. I did not really come back until we had children. I wanted them to be exposed to and experience something that once had been meaningful to me at their age. On this second encounter, God overpowered me. I found a relationship that filled a large void in my life. I tasted a love that I had always longed for. I knew I was on a journey, like the seekers after the holy grail. I would be searching for the rest of my life. Finally in recovery I have met a God that was always there in my religious tradition, but I did not see or hear that God as well as I did in recovery. In recovery I learned about not just having a relationship with God, but attempting to turn your life and your will over to the care of that God.

God constantly calls and waits for us and is faithful to us. God longs and yearns for us, and we are like the deer in Psalm 42 longing for that cool stream. I no longer worry when my children intermittently stop going to church or do not outwardly seem interested in a spiritual life. My experience is that God's steadfast love constantly calls them back. I know God waits for me, for them, and for you—and will do so through eternity.

Meditate on times in your life when God has been faithful to you when you felt like you least deserved it.

Psalm 118

**"I called to the LORD in my distress;
the LORD answered by setting me free."**

They both died within twenty-four hours of each other. One died alone. There was rarely anyone else there the few times I visited. The other died surrounded by his family and many friends. The death of the first was widely reported in the media and newspapers and on television. The other only had a very small obituary which appeared several days after he died. The first man had spent a life of perfection, making certain that procedures were carried out precisely the right way. The second man had been an alcoholic for much of his life. He had an awakening in a recovery center seven years before he died. He spent the rest of his life helping others find and stay in recovery. His was a life of progress not perfection. He died on his seventh AA birthday. That afternoon his AA friends brought a meeting to his house and gave him his seven-year AA coin. His daughter and his two grandchildren had made a birthday cake. The grandsons wanted to know why there was a number seven on Pops' birthday cake. "Isn't he 100 years old?" Pops laughed himself into a coughing fit when he heard that, as did all the friends and family in his room. After the meeting was over, he collapsed and died surrounded by those who loved him so dearly. His daughter writes, "Not a day goes by that we do not talk about him. The boys have asked if he will ever come back down from heaven."

I learned so much from these two very great men. From the first, I had a secondhand experience of the price of being right, of the ending to a life lived demanding perfection in yourself and others. From all accounts, his life as well as his ending was in isolation and lonely. From the second man I learned what happens when we live a life of relationship, of progress, not perfection. There will always be community to support us if we are only open to that relationship and are aware and accepting of our own humanness as well as the imperfection in our neighbor who is just like us. Daily we are given the choice of which life to try to live: progress or perfection. [12]

Pray today for progress rather than perfection in your life.

Psalm 119

"Turn my heart to your decrees,
and not to selfish gain.
Turn my eyes from looking at vanities;
give me life in your ways."

If you are a thinking person, I may sometimes drive you crazy. On the Myers-Briggs personality examination I am at one end of the scale towards the feeling function. That means relationships are very important to me. I make decisions by what is valuable rather than what is reasonable. I agonize when I am in conflict with someone. I often obsess about that person and what I should do to resolve the conflict, even when I do not particularly care for the person. When I do this, that person becomes the center of my life, my God. My most important relationship is with God. I must be accountable to God. God must be the Power I seek to please and stay with in relationship. I must try to find that inner voice of God in me, look and listen for it in others, and be guided by this relationship above all others. I must have concern for others, immediately make amends when I cause wrong, but not be obsessed by how I can stay in relationship to others, particularly when it involves playing into their and my own pathology.

I am also slowly becoming aware of a way God seems to heal me and bring me back into relationship with others — he allows me walk in their shoes or see the world from their perspective. I once worked with another physician whom I thought was incompetent. I could not understand her decision-making and methods of handling problems. One weekend I had to take over her job when she was on vacation. I was presented with the problems she saw daily. Overnight I was made aware of why she made the decisions she did.

Overnight I gained respect for her and her job. Overnight God transformed me.

Pray that you may be given new vision in difficult relationships as you examine the shoes others are walking in.

Psalm 120

**"Woe is me, that I am an alien in Meshech,
that I must live among the tents of Kedar."**

I believe Meshech is in Turkey and Kedar refers to Arabia. When our sons were in high school, we had an exchange student from Turkey living with us. This had not been in our original plans for that year. I always thought having an exchange student would be nice, but too much responsibility to add to our already hectic lives. Murat needed to exchange homes in the middle of the year and he had become a friend of one of our sons through soccer. This quiet, stoic student came to our home and changed our view of the world. Turkey is no longer a foreign country. There is a person named Murat whom we love now living there. When American troops were being sent to Arabia and Iraq, I not only feared for our sons' being involved in a conflict, but I feared for Murat and his country's border with Iraq. If only we could think in terms of persons and children and families in other countries instead of troops and arms. We also realized through Murat what a difference one person can make in our world view. I now find myself reading about the world news, not just our local news in our town and state.

Daily I find myself obsessing about the problems in my immediate life around me, the weather, our health, the conflicts our children are facing, that difficult person at work. Getting into relationship with someone from a different culture can be one of the most powerful ways of "getting out of ourselves" and our limited view of the world. My experience has been that relating to someone from another culture is one of the best ways to experience the promises[13]: We will lose interest in selfish things and gain interest in our fellows. Self-seeking will slip away. Our whole attitude and outlook upon life will change.[14]

Today intentionally get to know someone from another culture, another country.

Psalm 121

"The LORD will keep you from all evil;
he will keep your life.
The LORD will keep your going out and your coming in
from this time forth and for evermore."

My husband's father moved to a nursing home. Parts of many of his bones have been replaced with cancer, and in his weakness he has fallen and broken his hip. I watch our oldest son cut up his grandfather's meat and feed him and then gently wipe his mouth. My mind is flooded with memories of this same grandfather so similarly and caringly feeding his first grandson more than a quarter of a century earlier. I do not understand why such a gentle, God-loving man should suffer so many losses—his loving life-long companion, his health, his mind, his physical abilities. This is beyond my comprehension. But I do see in this alien environment the image of a loving God caring for his creation through three generations in a cyclic fashion. This image of God is the young and the strong feeding the weak and the old. My memory is the old and the strong feeding the young and the helpless. My prayer is that these two men will continue to grow and feed each other with love as they did that night. I also pray that I will not forget this memory of how God so lovingly continues to care for us in great adversity.

Return an act of kindness to someone who cared for you and loved you from your past.

Psalm 122

"For the sake of my relatives and friends
I will say, 'Peace be within you.' "

I have known someone for some time who is bitter about life and very unpleasant to be around. I do not look forward to visits. I put off calling because he is so unpleasant to talk to and usually comes out with some unkind or off-color remark. I do not know his whole story, but I know part of his resentment is that his father did not love him as much as his sister. I do not know if it was really true, but this is how he perceived the relationship. Unfortunately the human condition is that we will be dealt some difficult blows and we will also perform some unkindness that will harm others. This tragic figure is a reminder to me of how our wounds can destroy us. Our resentments for harm done, real or perceived, can dominate our lives and actually become God. I know it happens to me. Resentments for people who have harmed me become obsessions and dominate my actions and thoughts. One tool to help me get out of this dilemma is becoming aware that this person with whom I am having difficulty is now ruling my life. My only salvation is to pray for healing for both of us. I cannot change that person, but I can try to change how I react to him. I do not know of a sibling who at some time has not felt that he or she was less loved by his parents than his brother or sister. Literature and especially the Bible speak to this issue on many occasions. My experience has been that more often this is a perception rather than fact. However, there are times when parents cannot or are not capable of loving. My experience has been that God will always put someone — or often, many other people — in place of that parent to love that child. The difficulty for the child is to realize and accept that this is the parental love that was not available from the expected person. Many of us go through life still hoping that a parent will change rather than accepting that love from someone else. Some days we also may receive little glimpses of the awareness that our insatiable desire for this unconditional parental love can only be supplied by God.

Pray for a person you are carrying a resentment against. Pray that you will be changed.

Psalm 123

"Have mercy upon us, O LORD,
have mercy upon us,
for we have had more than enough of contempt."

This is a Psalm I often read in Lent. I remember this past Lent. I was very prepared, for this year I was given an overwhelming sense of my own self-centeredness. I looked into my mirror and saw the Wicked Witch from the *Wizard of Oz*. She even had that hideous greenish color and unkempt hair. Several co-workers and friends had also made me painfully aware of my many egocentric defects. Other sins had just become blatantly obvious. My world still centers around me and my priorities. I see these defects as excess baggage. I would like to get rid of this baggage, but it seems to be an intimate extension of my body. I am such a closure person. When I see a problem, I want it fixed. Now that I am painfully aware of some of my defects, I want them fixed—now. I am so proud that I finally can see some of my sins. Isn't awareness just enough? Eastern thought teaches us that the greatest sin is unawareness. Haven't I made great strides? Where is my reward for all this hard work and acceptance of who I am? Why won't God just fix me? I am aware and I want to be changed. I must now put myself in a position to be changed. Can I slow down my frantic pace of *doing* just long enough to put some of this baggage down? Am I afraid that there will not be a real person if this baggage is gone? I suddenly think about when I travel. I can barely make it to the next airport gate because of all my carry-ons. This may be very symbolic of my life. I envy those who travel with a small purse or one book. I must carry so much just in case I have time to work on this or that project. Perhaps the plane will be late and I will have nothing to do.

Imagine that you have been on a very long trip and have accumulated much too much luggage. You are racing to get home but can hardly move because of the weight of the luggage. Imagine that you slow down enough to at least briefly rest your baggage. Image yourself not picking up all that was put down when you begin your journey again. What is the essential luggage?

Psalm 124

"If it had not been the LORD who was on our side-let Israel now say-
if it had not been the LORD who was on our side,
when our enemies attacked us,
then they would have swallowed us up alive."

I repeatedly receive calls from a radiologist at a Children's Hospital about coming to Akron, Ohio to come and speak about work I have done with children with Sickle Cell Disease. I am trying to cut back on the busyness of my life and keep refusing. I don't want to go to Akron, Ohio. I feel like Jonah being called to Nineveh. I often go to a 12-step meeting at noon where there is a picture of the home in Akron of Dr. Bob Smith, one of the founders of the 12-step recovery program. I keep seeing that small brick-fronted house every day as I keep getting calls from the physician in Akron. I finally wonder if this just may be a message to go to Akron. I call back and say I will go on the condition that they will take me to Dr. Bob's house. Of course none of my hosts have heard of Dr. Bob. I go and Akron is a wonderful town that I almost missed seeing. I stay in a delightful hotel with rooms restructured from rounded silos that once were used for grain storage. I also think I was able to help one of the children there with Sickle Cell Disease. After the lectures I am taken to Dr. Bob's house, 855 Admore Avenue, modest, easily missed, tucked away in a quiet neighborhood. I go upstairs to the small bedroom where Dr. Bob met with Bill Wilson, a stock speculator from New York, on the day after Mother's Day in 1935. In this sparsely furnished upper room these two men eventually began a program, before I was born, to save my life and the lives of so many more. This is the work of God who is on our side. This is the God of my understanding: someone who loves us so dearly that there is a plan to care for and save us *before* we are born. Sitting in that house was one of the most powerful spiritual experiences I have known. I have an overwhelming sense of God's love for me and each of us manifested through two men I have never known but now want to remember.

Give thanks for people in your past who have pioneered in developing solutions to problems which have baffled you. Give thanks that their message has been brought to you by people in 12-step groups, in your church, or in any group that is supporting you.

Psalm 125

**"Those who trust in the LORD are like Mount Zion,
which cannot be moved, but abides forever."**

Trust and surrender are not one-time actions for me. I can surrender to God in the morning in my daily walk and meditation. I drive to work through a scenic part of town and listen to music or chants or meditations. I usually feel connected to God when I reach work. But as the cares of the day present, I often turn into a Mac truck going a full pace down a steep road. I soon have only my agenda in mind and become irritated by interruptions. I lose my connection to what my creator may have in mind for my day. If I do not have scheduled times during the day to stop and re-center, I literally lose it. I get into a pace where I cannot stop. I am exhausted at the end of the day, ready to seek some addiction—food, alcohol, relationships, spending, more work at home—to restore me to peace. I am learning about other options. Instead I could schedule a meeting with a friend, go to a 12-step meeting, stop during the day for meditation, walk again in the day, read, recite noonday prayers, attend a weekday worship service, or say intercessory prayers for other's needs to make some attempt to reconnect. I am reinventing the wheel. As I read about spiritual disciplines, I realize mine is a universal problem that many seem to have encountered through the ages. Most spiritual disciplines, eastern and western, have rules of life where oblates or participants in that rule are asked to make regular stops during the day to reconnect to God. I am drawn to the Hours that are kept in religious orders of regular prayer and worship during the day. Is there a possibility that we can be contemplatives in the midst of a busy day? This may be what T.S. Eliot called "the stillness in the dancing" in "Four Quartets." I read how others find spirituality in the workplace in John McQuiston's book, *Finding Time for the Timeless*. More and more I am drawn to regularly scheduled connections to God during my day. I know my only hope of peace is staying connected to God's presence during the day.

Write down your rule of life. Read about a rule of life from another spiritual discipline such as the Benedictine Rule.

Psalm 126

"May those who sow in tears reap with shouts of joy.
Those who go out weeping, bearing the seed for sowing,
shall come home with shouts of joy, carrying their sheaves."

I still remember the days after my mother died. The feeling of sadness was overwhelming. I had no energy, I had great difficulty focusing. My work became very difficult. I was expected to be back at work in usual form after a few days. I could not attain the frantic pace I worked at before. I was forced to say "no" to several issues. Perhaps this was a gift her death brought. I had to live life at a much slower rhythm — at least for a while. I began to treasure the slower pace.

Healing came slowly through the love of friends and family who almost literally carried me for days on a pallet like the paralytic of the New Testament carried by his friends to Jesus. Simple gestures of caring such as a call or a card had monumental meaning. Friends brought flowers and food and were role models for me of how to reach out in times of need. Other people whom I had known or worked with for over twenty years said nothing. I began to resent their inability to reach out to me in my time of great distress. Then by Grace I was given some insight into how terribly wounded they must be, so much so that they could not reach out. Their cup was empty. They, like me, had become so consumed by the busyness of their work that reaching out was not an option. It was not on their agenda. I am often there myself. I know well what it was like. I still travel to that place of busyness and self-involvement and often am unaware. Today I see through the glass darkly a little more clearly. Again I see my defects and self-centeredness most clearly by encountering the defects in others. I am usually blind to them in myself. I also am learning to find comfort by letting others know how much I am hurting rather than expecting them to know intuitively my sorrow. I also know my mother's death has left a big mothering hole in my life. Before she died, I tried to fill the hole with a relationship that could not be. After her death I expect my friends to fill the hole. I begin to have some awareness that this insatiable neediness is really my God hole and can be only filled by a mothering relationship from God. I am expecting and asking more of others than they can humanly give.

Give thanks for friends who have been with you in times of great difficulty. Pray for those who could not reach out because of their great wounding and busyness. Remember what it is like to be there. Remember that unreasonable expectations of others is usually from your need to fill your own God hole.

Psalm 127
**"It is in vain that you rise up early and go late to rest,
eating the bread of anxious toil."**

This is the story of my life, going from one busy
project to another, "eating the bread of anxious toil, rising
early, resting late." What am I trying to prove? Why is my life
so goal-oriented and obsessed with busyness? I cry out to God
for help. Am I trying to prove that I am capable and lovable?
Is it possible for me to change, to slow down? I am addicted to
busyness as if it were a drug. It seems to keep me from making
contact with God. It keeps me from living in the present. It
keeps me from dealing with and living in the now. It keeps me
from being open to the many times God tries to enter my life
during the day. I miss God's offerings during the day because
they were not on my busy agenda. Is it possible that I do not
need to do every project or task my mind brings to the
surface? Is it possible for me to learn boundaries and
discrimination? I am aware that the busyness in my head and
in my life keeps me from God. I also sense that I am not alone
in this misery. Working the 12-steps has given me awareness
of my addictions such as busyness and the promises hold out
healing.

Healing at present comes miraculously by using the
very defects which have driven me. I can only stop the
compulsion to keep doing by consistently scheduling in my
day times which will cut off the driver or the accelerator
pedal. At least once during the day I must religiously schedule
one of the activities that quiets my mind and releases my soul.
There are so many options: a walk, morning prayers,
meditation time, a 12-step meeting, a swim, exercise, a
worship service, a Eucharist, a women's group, a meal with
my family, lunch with a friend, playing with grandchildren,
writing time, playing music. These are the things which bring

me back to a quiet place where I can hear and feel that still small voice of the God of my understanding. These are no longer electives but essentials for survival. This is a start. Will I ever be able to schedule just "blank time" where I only wait for that still small voice? My instincts tell me that if I don't eventually do this, my physical body will abruptly schedule the down time.

Pray for yourself and others who are driven by busyness.

Psalm 128

"The LORD bless you from Zion.
May you see the prosperity of Jerusalem all the days of your life.
May you see your children's children.
Peace be upon Israel."

This Psalm was read by our younger son at a worship service celebrating our twentieth wedding anniversary. I remember my husband and I decided to celebrate our twentieth anniversary because we were not certain we could make it to the twenty-fifth. It was a joyous evening. Each of our three children had a part in the service, and then we all went out to the most elegant restaurant we knew about. That was over twenty-five years ago. I also remember reading this Psalm almost fifteen years ago in August when my husband and I left our daughter in California to go to college for the first time. Now our children have finished school, married and have their own children and careers. So much has happened to our family since that October evening—marriages, deaths, hardships, illnesses, graduations, awards, six grandchildren, wonderful trips—and we are still together. We are survivors. The words of the Psalm are still as powerful to me today as they were twenty-five years ago and as they must have been thousands of years of ago. I feel such gratitude for my husband, for my children, for our family who has stayed in relationship with each other in spite of many trials as well as much joy. I have been given the gift of commitment by those around me.

Make a gratitude list today for gifts given you by your family's love and support.

Psalm 129

"Often have they attacked me from my youth,
yet they have not prevailed against me,
...'The blessing of the LORD be upon you;
We bless you in the name of the LORD!' "

Today I am having difficulty dealing with life on life's terms. It seems as if I am being met by negative energy at every turn. "You didn't do that right. You forgot to take care of that problem we talked about. If you had done better in your job, we would not be in the mess we are in." I am overwhelmed. I begin to think of all the mistakes I have made and all the tasks in front of me. Step twelve tells us to carry our message of strength and hope to others. What do you do when you have no message, when your cup is empty? 12-step programs tell us when we start feeling alone, ungrateful, to reach out to someone else in the program. Call someone else. Go to a meeting. I am learning that this step applies to every part of my life when I am struggling with my own difficulties. A former priest who also was in a 12-step program modeled this for me. When his work at the church became overwhelming, when he kept hearing negative feedback, when he could no longer discern what was the next right thing, when his cup was empty, he would stop what he was doing and go visit someone in the hospital or someone who was homebound. I am forced to follow his example today. At my church, it is my day to visit patients in the hospital. All day I have been meeting one obstacle after another and receiving much criticism about my work. I am at a low energy state. I am too tired to do hospital visits, but go. I visit one of our church sextons whom I have not seen for some time since he suffered a stroke. His eyes brighten as do mine when we see each other after our long absence from each other. He tries to stand to greet me. We hold onto each other and instead sit face to face. I visit a couple I had never seen before with a new baby. Just seeing new life reminds me of the wonder of creation and the world. I visit a relative of a member of our church who has just had heart surgery. His presence reminds me of how precious and important each moment in our life is. It is amazing. I leave each room energized, knowing that I am doing the real ministry I am called to do, reaching out to others in need and at the same time, being healed by them. My problems no longer seem worth obsessing about. I begin to see what is really important in life: being in relationship with others, especially others that also have not had such a great day and are also struggling to be grateful. They help me fill back my cup with their kindness and gratitude and teach me that I as well have a very long gratitude list.

When you are having a difficult day, call or visit someone else you know may also be having difficulty. Listen to them and their story.

Psalm 130
"If you, O LORD, should mark iniquities, LORD, who could stand?
But there is forgiveness with you,
so that you may be revered."

The ugly beast reared up out of my inner swamp and breathed fire out of his nostrils—and in church of all places. That egocentric part of myself was raging. I was playing the prelude music on the harp at church. I had practiced for days. It was a great deal of trouble for my husband and me to bring the beautiful heavy instrument, the chair, the music, the stand, and extra strings out into the cool autumn morning. I had missed my favorite Sunday school class in order to get set up. The choir needed extra time to practice before the service and now there were only two minutes left for the harp music before church was to start. The lighting was unusually poor in the movie theater where St. Margaret's met. People were talking and moving all in front and around me as I played and they positioned themselves in their places for the service. The "star" in me was furious. All this work for such a little performance under such difficult conditions. I was nervous and mad at the same time—a rare combination. I did not like the resentments building up inside me. It took me hours to process all these feelings. My egocentric motives were showing. I was wearing them like my Sunday best. Usually I can hide this self centeredness under the quietness that only Southern women may know. I was not there as an offering to God but as a performer. Again, I am reminded of the 12-step saying that when our Ego is in control we are Edging God Out. I have an awareness that even a few minutes of having the opportunity to make a thank offering to God is a unique privilege. The obstacles to getting there were only signposts reminding me of the much greater roadblocks so many before us in our past overcame in order for us to connect today more easily to God. Perhaps I will handle this better next time.

Pray that God will heal that egocentric part of each of us.

Psalm 131

**"But I have calmed and quieted my soul,
like a weaned child with its mother;
my soul within me is like a weaned child."**

I still clearly see a young four-year-old patient I cared for almost thirty years ago. Laura was small for her age and ravaged with a deadly tumor, neuroblastoma. Do I remember her so well because she was my daughter's age? I see her sunken blue eyes and the blonde hair that came and went with her chemotherapy. I remember just as vividly Laura's mother, who watched her beautiful daughter suffer through a long and painful death. I particularly remember Laura's last Easter weekend. She was lying beneath a large nuclear medicine camera to monitor her recent bone metastases. She was wearing an Easter corsage of yellow roses and baby's breath pinned to her tiny yellow robe. Her mother sang softly as she held her daughter's frail, pain-ridden body quiet for the study. As she almost surrounded Laura with her body, she, too, was engulfed by the imposing medical camera above both of them. That scene will always remind me of the God of my understanding who cares for those who suffer. God takes the test with us. God surrounds us with love, gets under the camera with us, weeps with us, gives us yellow roses to wear even in the midst of our suffering, and sings softly in our ear.[15]

If you are struggling with physical, spiritual, or mental pain, remember Laura and how God is holding you.

Psalm 132

"I will not enter my house or get into my bed;
I will not give sleep to my eyes or slumber to my eyelids,
Until I find a place for the LORD."

I rise early this morning before work. I take a slow meditative walk through my neighborhood on this early spring day. The sun is just coming up. Birds are singing. Red bud, forsythia, daffodils, are peeking out all over my path. I come home to my living-room, light incense, say Morning Prayer, and imagine my prayers rising with the fragrant smoke. I listen to Marion Woodman tapes about the feminine and masculine on my way to work. I have a delicious breakfast after I arrive. I am ready. By afternoon I am caught up in a hectic pace of constant demands and constant needs. Everything must be done right away. I am the only one working. Everyone else is sitting around eating bonbons. No one else is working as hard as I am. I am carrying the burdens of the world. The world again revolves around me. Finally I lose it. I am sharp with someone who is only trying to help — but she is not helping as fast as I want her to. All of my preparations from the morning to stay centered with God have been of no help. I am back in the same place I was years ago before recovery. I am working at a frantic pace that only a superwoman could sustain. I have lost my connection to the source of my energy.

I realize that often I am still trying to stay connected to God so that God will allow me to accomplish what is on my agenda. I am slowly learning that that my agenda may be different from what God has planned for me. My meditations, my prayers, my walks, my centering are not to quiet my soul so that I can perform monumental tasks. They are tools to place me in position to receive and connect to God. All of these disciplines are containers to hold or receive God's presence, not tools to accomplish Herculean pursuits. I will lose that connection when I begin to believe that I am in charge of the world.

What are the things you do in your life to produce a container for God to connect to your life? How do you use your container?

Psalm 133

"How very good and pleasant it is when kindred live together in unity!
It is like the precious oil on the head, running down upon the beard, on the beard of Aaron,
running down over the collar of his robes.
It is like the dew of Hermon,
which falls on the mountains of Zion.
For there the LORD ordained his blessing, life forevermore."

My husband and I walk into St. Alban's Church in Washington and immediately feel at home. St. Albans is next to the spacious grounds of the National Cathedral, and the familial architecture is so reminiscent of where I worship in Little Rock at Trinity Cathedral. We are attending church with my cousin Linda and her husband Dennis whom we see once or twice a year on visits to Washington. Linda is a beautiful person, a breast cancer survivor whose mother died of breast cancer. Linda still has active disease but leads an amazingly full life.

Linda and I played together as children. Our grandmothers were sisters, best friends, and often lived together. Our mothers were close as well and lived near each other until they died. Some people say that Linda and I look enough alike to be sisters.

As we wait for the organ prelude Linda turns and whispers to me that when she goes into her chemotherapy sessions each week, she carries with her something of her mother's, her mother's wedding ring, a piece of clothing or jewelry.

I am flooded with memories of women in our family down through the centuries worshipping together and walking and sitting beside each other through difficult journeys. I feel our grandmothers, our mothers, and women in our past whose names we do not know present beside us. I also feel the future, our daughters and nieces and grandchildren with us. St. Albans like Trinity Cathedral is a holy place where the prayers of so many in our past and in our future permeate the walls and whisper in our ears the love and connection of the peace that passes understanding. We are never alone if we only have ears to hear and eyes to see.

The prelude begins and even that is a familiar one as well. I am at home. [16]

Pray that you may stay in relationship to members of your family. Pray for God's grace to be able to do so.

Psalm 134

"Come, bless the LORD, all you servants of the Lord."

There are many days I read the Psalms and I do not feel like blessing the God of my understanding or giving thanks or praise. I am not in the mood. Our loving God gives me so much freedom and at the same time seems constantly to be sending me little wake-up calls, some subtle, some loud, to remind me what this life is all about. The Psalms are a daily wake-up call. God sends me wake-up calls in the events of my own life and those of others. Most of the time, however, I do not see these messages. I am too busy working out my own agenda. I ignore them, or deny them, or think they are for someone else — not me. My younger brother recently had a mild stroke and is recovering. He has another chance for a different life with more attention to his body with diet and exercise. We all need to hear that message as well. His illness is a reminder of how tenuous our life is. I have a spiritual friend who lets me know when I am ignoring my family or my friends or when my work consumes me. I know she tells me this because she cares for me. She has nothing to gain by letting me know her observations. In times past when my husband had complained about my busyness, I would react by listing some of his faults or justifying the need for me to do all these important things. I am slowly learning that I should pay more attention to these messages from him and make some change in my daily patterns when he sees me out of balance.

Daily we see unhappiness in so many lives. We see friends losing lifelong companions, friends with serious illnesses. It should always be a call for us to be thankful for so many loving people and the present health and happiness we have in our lives. We take so much of what God has given us for granted: a loving companion, beautiful, talented, healthy children or grandchildren, a fulfilling profession, many exciting interests, treasured friends. My prayers this morning are that we all will be more aware of the undeserved and tenuous gifts we have received in our lives and that we will hear these wake-up calls and appreciate and share the many blessings we have been given.

Today sing or say praises to the God of your understanding for the many blessings you have been given. Let at least one family member or friend know how much you care about them. Be open to God's wake-up calls to get you back on the path of the life God has created for you.

Psalm 135

"Praise the LORD!
...you that stand in the house of the LORD,
in the courts of the house of our God.
Praise the LORD,
for the LORD is good."

I remember my first trip to Greece. Our guide on Rhodes tells me about a small Greek church just beneath our hotel. I never would have known it was a church. It was very carefully hidden by the spring hibiscus, red roses, orange trees, pomegranate and olive trees in its courtyard. Its Greek name means "The Revelation of the Highest of All." I am overcome by darkness as I enter the small, poorly lit chapel. Then I sense the smell of incense. As my eyes adapt from the strong sunlight, I begin to see the beautiful walls ornately covered with colorful paintings of saints. There is a single candle and bread in a basket left over from the morning Eucharist. Ribbons hang from chandeliers. I wonder if this may be part of the celebration of the present Easter season. Holy books and silver Bibles are placed on large stands. There are little plaques or tamata hanging under a large silver icon of Mary holding Jesus. There are pictures on the plaques representing babies, children, and body parts such as legs, ears, and eyes. I am told the tamata are placed there in thanksgiving for healing of whatever is depicted in the pictures. A Greek couple come in and circle the church and reverently kiss many of the icons as they seem to be reciting prayers. I am moved by the sacredness of the church and these two people. I realize that we in our western culture have lost some of the reverence for the beauty, the holiness, the awe, the mystery of God in our attempt not to worship the beautiful icons or other objects of worship. We may have thrown out some of the baby with the bath water. I pray that I can take back home this awe and reverence and thanksgiving for the presence of the holiness of the God of my understanding.

If you were to hang in a sacred place a picture of what has been healed by God in your life, what would be in the picture?

Psalm 136

"It is he who remembered us in our low estate,
for his steadfast love endures forever;
and rescued us from our foes,
for his steadfast love endures forever."

I am learning that my foes are inside of me. I pray to be rescued from what often seems like insanity in my life. Friends in 12-step groups talk about insanity as "doing the same thing over and over and expecting different results." Today I find much insanity in my life. I have the same eating patterns but expect to lose weight. I am especially insane about time. I think I can get accomplished in ten minutes what should take twenty or thirty minutes, so I am often late. I think I can perform one more errand or project before I go on to my next patient or appointment. I honestly used to believe that if the day had twenty-five instead of twenty-four hours that I would get all my jobs accomplished. My inability to get everything accomplished was not my fault, but it was the fault of God who did create enough hours in the day. I have changed very little over the years. I may take this character defect with me to the grave—or it may drive me to the grave. One thing is different—at least I am a little more aware of my behavior and some of its insanity. The problem is me, not the world. My prayers are daily that the God of my understanding will change me. Sometimes God and my body must hit me broadsides to make the change. I have developed some arthritis in my feet. It has made me slow down my lifestyle considerably. Some days when I stop feeling sorry for myself, I have flashes of delight that I might even enjoy this slower pace.

Pray that we will be made aware of the insanity in our lives.
Pray that we will have courage to change our behavior.

Psalm 137
"How shall we sing the LORD's song in a foreign land?"

Work sometimes seems like a foreign land. I can sing praises, be thankful in my daily meditation time, but what do I do when I get up from my sacred space and go to work? How do I carry my connection with God to the work place—or even more difficult, how do I keep my connection with God at work? Once I get started on my own agenda for the day, God seems to leave me—or I lose that fine silken thread-like connection I had with my creator. I am on my time, not God's time. I try to stop in the middle of the day for prayers, but usually I put it off until I can get the current problem solved. This ends up being never, for soon there is a new problem and no time. My only salvation is if I purposely schedule time in the day for a reminder of my need for God's presence in my life. I try at least to pray some of the prayers of the hours at noon and in the evening and night using Phyllis Tickle's *Divine Hours*. I try to schedule a luncheon meeting with one or more spiritual or recovery friends who get me back on track during midday. Also I am learning a little about the many interruptions during the day—phone calls, unexpected visits from friends, colleagues, patients, my husband, relatives, children. I am slowly learning not to take these as interruptions but as possible opportunities again to make a God connection. In the past, I would be annoyed, telling friends who would call that I was just too busy and would talk later. I don't know if each interruption is a message from God, but I am considering that each attempt at change in my agenda might be God trying to intervene in my life. I am at least making an effort to be aware and listen instead of constantly being annoyed that my plan has been interrupted.

Today have lunch with a soul friend. Talk about your many interruptions during the day. Consider if some may be God letting you know how much you are loved through a friend. Consider the possibility that the annoying interruption may be a message to change direction.

Psalm 138

"The LORD will fulfill his purpose for me;
your steadfast love, O LORD, endures forever.
Do not forsake the work of your hands."

We meet our son, John, and two of his children in Memphis to return his older son who has spent the week with us in Little Rock. Our son lives in Nashville and Memphis is a good halfway dropping-off place between Little Rock and Nashville. We meet at the Pink Palace Museum and have a wonderful reunion watching our grandchildren see the exhibits of what the past was like millions of years ago up to a century ago. We loved the exhibits of Memphis a hundred years ago, scenes from the medical school in Memphis where my husband and I graduated and past physicians we had once heard about, as well as the first Piggly Wiggly grocery store in Memphis. We talk to our grandchildren about the yellow fever epidemic in Memphis and the nuns from St. Mary's Cathedral where my husband and I were confirmed and our two sons were baptized. We remembered that the nuns lost their lives during the epidemic caring for others.

Our son tells us as he leaves that he is taking his children by to see his grandparents' home and their gravesite in Memphis. My husband's parents have been dead for some time, but our son wants to honor them and the memories he had visiting them in Memphis when he was growing up in Little Rock. We say that is nice, but we must return home for we must prepare for another trip the next day. When we return to Little Rock, we receive an excited call from our son. He not only was able to drive by their house and show it to his children, but sees a neighbor out in the yard with her grandchildren. The neighbor recognizes John and talks about how she misses his grandparents and remembers his visits. She then takes him and his three children over to his grandparents' house and introduces them to the new owners. The present owners give them a tour of the home and the yard. Over the phone he excitedly tells us about all the changes. Then John describes taking his children to his grandparents' grave site and putting flowers over their physical resting place. His children ask many questions: "Are they really under the ground where we are walking? Will you tell us more about them?"

As we hang up the phone, we are also flooded with memories of my husband's parents who were such an important part of our lives, who modeled for us the unconditional love for others that comes from a relationship with God. We remember how much we miss them and give thanks for the privilege of having them as family.

This is not how we started out this day. We had only planned to return our grandson to his parents. In addition, we took an historical trip of millions of years ago to just a few years ago. We learn how our children teach us how to honor the past and carry it on to their children. We also are reconnected to a past we were a part of and feel a little stronger connection to a past we never knew.

I am reminded that when I was growing up each Sunday I went with my grandparents to the cemetery in my small home town to put flowers on their parents' and grandparents' graves. This is where I heard stories about their family as well as people my grandparents had known when they were growing up as we walked the grounds of the cemetery and looked at the new and worn markers, the statue of a little dog by the grave of his owner, the angel at the foot of the grave of a child, the simple military marker of a dead soldier. Learning and telling stories about our past connects us to a world bigger than our own and perhaps also connects us to that steadfast love of our God that connects us all. Our son has reminded us that visiting cemeteries and old houses can be places where old love stories can once again come alive.

Visit a place where you are connected to good memories from a past time that will help you remember God's steadfast love.

Psalm 139

"You search out my path and my lying down,
and are acquainted with all my ways...
Where can I go from your spirit?
Or where can I flee from your presence?"

I have a little glimmer through the glass darkly of the way God works in my life, how God constantly calls and cares for me. God was a central part of my life in my growing up years, instilled by a social system as well as an extrinsic need for help from some power greater than what was in me and around me. When I went to college, I was exposed to a new system, a new intellectual world. All the power I needed was inside of me or I could attain it by persistence and hard work. My grandfather was the most important person in my childhood. He took me to church, walked with me in the woods and along riverbanks, read the funnies to me before I could read, and gave me a nickel for ice cream when I visited his jewelry shop on my way home after school. I was sustained by his unconditional love. I rarely saw him after I left home for college, but I was still sustained by the love he gave me. When he died twenty years later, I was devastated. I could only bear the loss by believing that I would see him again. I had to believe that there was something beyond death. Therefore I renewed my relationship with God with vigor in order to endure the pain of my loss. The religion I sought, however, was not that of my Baptist grandfather. I was drawn to the Anglican tradition, so very different from the beliefs of the southern Baptist. I was drawn not by what my grandfather believed, or what he said he believed, but by how he loved me. God used my grandfather's love to bring me back to him, but the God I found was not in the same tradition of my grandfather's.

I intermittently think of my children and their own faith. Some are following a religious or spiritual tradition similar to ours; others are not. My experience tells me not to be concerned. Our major ministry to our children and to others is the love we show them, not necessarily what we tell them we believe. Some say love is an action not a feeling.

Give thanks for those who, in their love for you, show and teach you the love that comes from God.

Psalm 140

"Those who surround me lift up their heads;
let the mischief of their lips overwhelm them!
Let burning coals fall on them!
Let them be flung into pits, no more to rise!"

Today I really identify with the Psalmist. Sometimes I become so angry at people I feel have unfairly treated me or my loved ones that I would not mind if a few burning coals came their way! I think this is part of the greatness of the Psalms: they express so many human feelings, some we are not proud of, many which are not thought of as "Christian." These are real people writing the Psalms, not stylized or idealized characters. Each day I learn a little more about the resentments the Psalmist talks about which I carry for wrongs done to me by other people. I still carry resentments towards people who harmed me in my childhood as well as unfair treatment I received yesterday and today. I am realizing that as long as I carry this resentment, this person is still hurting me. It is not just the one-time event that has wounded me. The same wrong continues to wound me in my mind and body. The wound never heals. As I nurse this resentment, this person becomes my God, for I let that person live rent free in my head for much of the day and night. As long as I keep this resentment, this hate, in my mind and body, I am being destroyed. I cannot grow. This knowledge is an incentive to me to learn to forgive people for wrongs they have done to me. I only want the wrong to hurt me for that one event, not for the rest of my life. Forgiveness is my only chance at healing.

In your prayers, make a conscious effort to forgive someone who has harmed you.

Psalm 141

"I call upon you, O LORD; come quickly to me;
give ear to my voice when I call to you.
Let my prayer be counted as incense before you,
and the lifting up of my hands as an evening sacrifice."

The phone rings. I reach to pick up my portable phone. It is not there. I miss the call and frantically begin to search for the phone in my office, the bedroom, the living room, the kitchen. I feverously dial my number and listen for the hidden ring. I do not hear it. (I learn later from more technically savvy friends that I should have used the page button on my phone base to find the phone, but alas, I did not know at the time.) I go to rooms in my house I have not been in for days. I even go out on the porch that is still covered with ice. The longer I search, the more upset I get. I am losing my mind. How can anyone forget where she has left her phone? I start fantasizing that other people, my husband, my children, the cleaning people, have used my phone and have left it somewhere. It is not possible that I could lose my phone. Finally in exhaustion, I go to bed knowing I will never see my phone again. I wonder what else I will lose tomorrow. As I lie there, my mind quiets, I retrace my steps the day before, the last time I used the phone. I was in the kitchen talking to our younger son. After I talked to him, I remember looking for some old pictures of our grandchildren in a basket in our kitchen. A voice says, "Get up and look in the basket in the kitchen." In my mind, I answer, "I am tired, I have already looked there." I spend a restless night. The next morning, I get up depressed that I have been so careless to lose my phone. Again, I think, someone else has taken it. After some time, I remember the voice in the night, "Look in the basket." I go to the kitchen and as you might imagine, there is my phone, in the basket hidden under old pictures.

I put finding my lost phone at the top of my gratitude list. Then on my way to work, I contemplate what I have learned. The voice in the night reminded me of the voice I heard when I was caught in my addiction. That night, that voice said, "You need help or you will lose your job, your family, and your life." I have heard so many other people talk about that voice that brought them to a moment of clarity about their addictions and led them to recovery. Some would call it the unconscious, some call it the subconscious, some call it the voice of logic in our heads, some call it Grace, some call it the Holy Spirit. Whatever it is, I believe that voice in my life is a still, small voice that comes most often when my mind is quieted. It speaks the truth in love. I believe it is God lovingly trying to get through my panicked mind.

Contemplate on a moment of clarity you've experienced. Consider that moments of clarity from God may continue to come to you daily if you are open to them.

Psalm 142
"When my spirit is faint,
you know the way...
For you will deal bountifully with me."

One of our sons returned to Little Rock after he graduated from college to enter medical school for four years and then complete a four-year surgical residency in ear, nose, and throat. My husband and I experienced the unbelievable blessing to be able to relate to him and his new wife on a daily basis. My husband retired from his medical practice when they had their first child, Langley, in order to help care for her. Our life was enriched by relating to our children as adults and learning and giving unconditional love that only grandparents know. Our world soon centered on spending time with our grandchildren as they arrived, taking them to school, to plays, to concerts, baby sitting, taking them on trips and excursions, reading to them, watching movies with them, walking with them along the river, going to their school plays, taking them to music lessons, putting them to bed, having them over for sleepovers.

At the end of our son's residency, he found a job in another city and he and his wife and now three children moved away. Our world was devastated. We no longer related on a daily basis to what had become the center. Our grandchildren were far enough away that we could only see them about once every other month. There are still days when we miss them so much. I can now understand why grandparents can uproot their entire lives they have known for most of their life in order to move to be closer to grandchildren.

From this experience I have learned how change is a constant. I have learned to try to appreciate every day I am in relationship with people I care about. I have also learned how to relate to our grandchildren from a distance in a new way. We see them and call as often as we can. Today as I pass by the turn off to the school we once drove them to or their first house or a playground we often went to, instead of feeling sad, I have learned to say a prayer of thanksgiving for that time we had together and pray for our grandchildren today. I pray for them and what they are doing today even though we will not be as involved. I am learning about how to stay connected in prayer. Every day God uses our grandchildren to teach me a new way to live, in effect to live the Serenity Prayer, accepting what I can not change but changing how I react to the change.

Pray the Serenity Prayer today. Meditate on changes in your life you can not change. Mediate on how you can change your reaction.

Psalm 143

**"Do not enter into judgment with your servant,
for no one living is righteous before you."**

I harshly judged a partner today because she did not treat an African-American patient and her child with the courtesy and respect I thought she should have. My partner was late for the procedure, never apologized, and was impatient with the scared child and anxious mother. My partner had a long agenda today, and the uncooperative child she was working with was putting her more behind in her schedule. My partner was not treating her patient the way she would have wanted to be treated. Later in the day, unbelievably, I found myself in the same behavior pattern. My inconsideration was to a wealthier family. The mother had been trying through several channels to get in touch with me about her child. I sent messages through intermediaries instead of talking to her myself. I was too busy. My time was too important. I knew this was an informed, demanding mother, and she would have many questions, some I might not be able to answer. My partner showed prejudice to the poor, I did it to the well to do and informed. I am slowly learning to be a little less judgmental. The very character defects I see in my friends, I also see in myself, sometimes in the same situation or some variation. We all have our intolerances. God allows us to see them in ourselves usually through seeing them in others first.

Pray for an awareness of your intolerances and prejudices today. If you are having difficulty, look for them first in others. Do not judge, only observe. Soon you may see them in yourself. Pray for the courage to change yourself.

Psalm 144

"May our sons in their youth be like plants full grown,
our daughter like corner pillars cut for the structure of a
palace."

I remember reading this Psalm the day we took our
younger son to college in Tennessee for the first time. Our van
was jam-packed with all his treasures, microwave, rugs,
chairs, desks, books, refrigerator, linens, and clothes. There
was great excitement in participating in a passage of such
magnitude. He was our most independent child, but even he
showed some signs of anxiousness about his new life. I think
he was most worried about whether he would succeed or not.
Words cannot express what I wished I could say to him. There
was so much I wanted to tell my son. As I worked through it
in my mind, my thoughts sounded preachy, parental. I
wanted him to know that we were trying to accept him as an
adult. We wanted him to be successful in finding God's plan
for his life and have the courage to carry it out. We wanted
him to know we loved him as unconditionally as parents can.
Would he hear me when we said, "Use your talents, but our
love for you is not dependent on your success"? Has he
learned from us both the parable of the talents and the parable
of the prodigal son?[17]

*Pray for children leaving home to attend school, begin work,
or begin new families. May our community swell with new
life and may we support them with our love.*

Psalm 145

**"The Lord upholds all who are falling,
and raises up all who are bowed down.
The eyes of all look to you,
and you give them their food in due season."**

I meet regularly with a 12-step group who have had a painful awareness that their lives were heading in the wrong direction in their addiction. They are now are trying to lead a more spiritual, less egocentric life without the addiction. A new person, Lloyd, comes in this month. He is cold and hostile and often leaves before the meeting is over. He exudes negative energy. I do not like to hear what he says or be around him. This week I am late and the only empty seat is next to Lloyd and I sit down. I am called on, I speak, and then I call on Lloyd because I do not know who else has spoken. After the meeting, he thanks me for calling on him and asks how I am doing. Since that meeting he has gone out of his way to reach out to me.

John Stone Jenkins tells us that others cannot reach out with love if their cup is empty. Only when their cup has been filled with love can they also give love to another. Lloyd had a very empty cup. In my mind, I only filled his a little, but then he seemed to overflow with love. A very small act of kindness that was not even intentional sent back overwhelming love.

I also know that kindness is catching. Yesterday as I drove in our driveway, I noticed our postman across the street. He had just delivered the mail to our neighbor whose husband tragically died last year. Before leaving her mailbox, our postman brought up to the street our neighbor's garbage cans and trash for the next day's delivery. I mentioned to him that he had a "big delivery." He commented, "If I show some small kindness to someone in need, perhaps someone will remember me when I am in need." I found myself following through on some small acts of kindness later in the day, leaving a flower for a friend on her desk, letting someone from a side street get in front on me on the way out to dinner.

I also know others who have such an empty cup that no kindness seems to affect them. I may constantly try to send kindness to them and nothing or very little returns. I do not understand. Are their wounds so great that their cup is bottomless? I do know that I get into trouble when I start looking for results when I offer love to others. It is better to have no expectations, offer it as a free gift, and wait for the surprises to happen when I least expect them. This is very difficult, but the unexpected return of unconditional love, as I received from Lloyd, is God's gift back to us. Observing others doing acts of kindness like our postman also is a gift from God. They are constant reminders of the need for us consciously and unconsciously to give away this love.

Reach out today to someone you sense is lonely by a small act of kindness. Do not expect results. Give your love as unconditionally as you can.

Psalm 146

"Praise the LORD!
Praise the LORD, O my soul!
I will praise the LORD as long as I live;
I will sing praises to my God all my life long."

More and more in my journey through the Psalms I receive little glimpses of what most brings peace to the Psalmist and perhaps also to me. Why are so many Psalms filled with praise to God? Why is this praise such a constant, daily part of the worship in Jewish, Moslem, Christian, and other traditions? Peace comes from gratitude to our Creator for what we are given. This has been my experience. It seems to be ever-present in the Psalms. When I am grateful for what I have and recognize God as my creator and sustainer, I am at peace. When I give thanks for improvement in an illness, no matter how minor, I receive peace. When I give thanks for a procedure that went well, a conference or meeting that was not as difficult as I expected, I find peace. When I give thanks for so many friends who lift me up in times of trouble, I find peace. When I am having difficulty with life, a spiritual friend always suggests to me to make a gratitude list. Sometimes I am furious with her for suggesting such a thing in my time of great misery. Hasn't she learned anything new in all the years we have known each other! However, this always gets me back on the right track. Depression leaves as I remember the good in my life that has been blinded by hard times. I seem to find that connection back to the God of my understanding by giving thanks, and the peace comes when that connection returns.

Make a gratitude list for today.

Psalm 147

"For he strengthens the bars of your gates;
he blesses your children within you.
He grants *peace* within your borders."

What brings peace within your borders? As a deacon in my religious tradition, I often send people out at the end of our worship service with the words, "Go in peace to love and serve the Lord." Where is this peace that should go out with us? I have sought it in work, relationships with other people, fame, prestige, food, clothes, material things, alcohol, control, power. These are dead ends. Sometimes it has taken me longer to realize the emptiness in each of these lifestyles than others. Many times I still go back to one or many to try it one more time with the fantasy of a different result, especially those that are socially acceptable.

The only lasting peace comes from a continuous turning over of my life to God. This is easier said than done. There are many tools that God has given us to surrender to his care. We have talked about many of them in these meditations on the Psalms: prayer, meditation, 12-step meetings, living the 12-steps, daily reviewing harms we have done and making amends, following a rule of life, reaching out to others. There are even more that God will reveal to each of us if we are open. Before we can take action, we must be open and aware of the message God is revealing to us through the disciplines of our lives, through Nature and the world outside of our own, through others, and through that still small voice.

Make a conscious effort today to sit outside or by a window and listen and look for the peace that God has to offer in your life.

Psalm 148

"Praise the LORD!
 Praise the LORD from the heavens;
Praise him, all his angels...
Praise him, sun and moon:
praise him, all you shining stars!
Praise him, you highest heavens,
and you waters above the heavens!"

We are at the beach and arrive home in time to watch the sunset. It is November and the sun sets close to five o'clock in the evening over the ocean. No matter what mood I am feeling, I am always uplifted by watching the sunrise or sunset. Tonight's sunset is especially spectacular. It has been a rainy, cool day. Mist rises from the sea and large cloudbanks cover most of the sky. The sun moves like a ballerina through the cloudbanks. She rhythmically makes brief shining appearances in small openings between the clouds and is brilliantly reflected on the sea below. The sky is alive with shades of pink and orange. I run for my camera. I want to hold on to it, capture the event. In looking for my camera, I miss part of the spectacle. Each moment is beautiful and different in its own right. It will never be the same again. As the clouds move through the falling sun, different bands of this great round ball make unusual patterns across the horizon. This is my best exercise in learning to live in the moment. If I do not constantly stay with the moment, I miss a great deal. How many sunsets have I missed because I was too busy looking for my camera or because I had more important things to do?

I am overcome with the beauty of this earth, the greatness of God's gifts to us—so many gifts we miss seeing daily. I am overcome with gratitude for the goodness of the God of our understanding. I don't want to miss any more of it.

Stop and find a place to watch the sunset tonight.

Psalm 149

"Let Israel be glad in its Maker;
let the children of Zion rejoice in their King.
Let them praise his name with dancing,
making melody to him with tambourine and lyre.
For the LORD takes pleasure in his people."

We attended the fortieth birthday celebration of our former church home. I was greeted by a dear friend with, "Welcome home." Another old friend gave us flowers as we left. We were hugged with love by so many old friends. Indeed I learned that day what homecoming was all about. Our old pew was on the front row of the west transept, where we could see all the action. We started sitting there when our children were in choir so we could keep an eye on them. They are now married with children of their own. It was very comfortable to sit there again. I was deeply moved as I watched our former priest lovingly offer the Eucharist to the flock he had released ten years previously. I cried with joy as I saw him at the rail bless the children of children I knew he had baptized and prepared for confirmation. After the service, we went to the columbarium garden in the churchyard and remembered old friends from this parish who had died, especially two members who sat on our pew. My heart overflows with gratitude and praise for the people of God who worship him in that house. We have all been so cared for by a loving power greater than ourselves.[18]

Give thanks today for any spiritual traditions that have nurtured you.

Psalm 150
"Let everything that breathes praise the LORD! Praise the LORD!"

What is the call of the Psalms? Why have they changed lives, brought comfort, and restored us for centuries? Why are they a constant part of every Christian Rule of Life? Why have they brought healing to those with lives too busy and tumultuous to see or find God? I have tried to be healed by other means in my too-busy, workaholic, addictive lifestyle: food, alcohol, spending, shopping, exercise, relationships. Each of these has been a Band-Aid to cool down or soothe my racing mind and agenda. They all work for a while to turn off the committee in my mind that wants to do more and more. But then there is a point where they no longer work. The need for them becomes just as powerful as the drive to busyness. The cure has become part of the disease. The Psalms are not a Band-Aid, but a guidepost to a redirection of my life. They are icons calling out to me that our purpose is to serve and praise a God who "delights in us." Our only hope for peace is to listen for this connection with our Creator. The world tells us to strive for success, power, accomplishments, projects, goals. The Psalms call to us to strive for our relationship with God on a daily, hourly, momentary basis. Listening and living a life of praise and gratitude is a new life for me. It is a road less traveled. To the best of my knowledge, it is the journey I think the God of my understanding has chosen for us. I share my journey with you and look forward to hearing more of your journey.

Today share what the Psalms have meant to you with someone else.

It is easy to go through life looking feverishly for special ways to find God when God is most of all to be found in doing common things with uncommon conscientiousness.

-- Joan Chittister, *The Rule of Benedict: Insights for the Ages*

Index of Subjects by Psalm

Notes

[1] *Big Book of Alcoholics Anonymous*, p.63.

[2] Georges de La Tour's "The Repentant Magdalene" can be found at
     www.nga.gov/fcgi-bin/tinfo_f?object=54386

[3] Originally appeared in the *Arkansas Episcopalian*, Vol. 66, No. 5, June, 1992.

[4] Originally appeared in the *Arkansas Episcopalian*, Vol. 64, No. 4, September, 1990.

[5] Originally appeared in *The Living Church*, Vol. 210, No. 15, April 9, 1995.

[6] Originally appeared as "Going Home" in *WomenPsalms,* compiled by Julia Ahlers, Rosemary Broughton, and Carl Koch, St. Mary's Press, 1992, pp. 66-67.

[7] *Big Book of Alcoholics Anonymous*, 4th Edition, pp. 83-84.

[8] Originally appeared in the *Arkansas Episcopalian*, Vol. 63, No. 4, May 1989.

[9] *Big Book of Alcoholics Anonymous,* 4th Edition, p. 84.

[10] Originally appeared in *Healing Presence,* Joanna Seibert, Temenos Publishing, 2007, pp. 143-145.

[11] Originally appeared in *Healing Presence,* Joanna Seibert, Temenos Publishing, 2007, pp. 9-10.

[12] Originally appeared in *Healing Presence,* Joanna Seibert, Temenos Publishing, 2007, pp. 100-101.

[13] *Big Book of Alcoholics Anonymous*, 4th Edition, p. 84.

[14] Originally appeared in *Forward Day by Day*, August, 1992, p. 19.

[15] Originally appeared in *Healing Presence,* Temenos Publishing, 2007, pp. 15-16.

[16] Originally appeared in *Healing Presence,* Temenos Publishing, 2007, pp. 26-27.

[17] Originally appeared in *Forward Day by Day*, August, 1992, p. 23.

[18] Originally appeared in *Forward Day by Day*, August, 1992, p. 5.

Acknowledgments

Cover photograph of Dr. Seibert by Sean Moorman.
www.seanmoormanphoto.com

Scripture readings are from the New Revised Standard
Version of the Bible unless otherwise indicated.

Cover art by Mitchell Crisp.

Graphic design by Patrick Burnett
www.patrickburnett.com

Front cover photograph taken by Dr. Seibert of the Good
Shepherd in the chapel of the Good Shepherd at the
Washington National Cathedral.

Dr. Joanna Seibert is a professor of radiology and pediatrics at Arkansas Children's Hospital and the University of Arkansas Medical Sciences. She has been an ordained deacon in the Episcopal Diocese of Arkansas for eight years. She is presently assigned to Trinity Cathedral Little Rock. She has recently written a book, Healing Presence, about visiting the sick and dying and grieving. She also edited a book of meditations on the Eucharistic readings, Surrounded by a Cloud of Witnesses, has been a writer for Forward, Day by Day, and is a frequent contributor to the Living Church and the Anglican Digest. She and her husband, Robert, for eight years were Arkansas' representatives to the National Cathedral in Washington. She is a facilitator for the Community of Hope, Walking the Mourner's Path and Trinity's health ministry. She is also on the board of the National Recovery Ministries of the Episcopal Church. She was named one of three "women of distinction" in Arkansas in 1992 and has been named one of the top 100 women in Arkansas by Arkansas Business for several years as well as being on the list of outstanding doctors in the country for many years. She is a former president and chairman of the board of the Society for Pediatric Radiology. Arkansas Children's Hospital annually gives an award to the physician at the hospital who embodies teamwork in his or her practice. The award is named the Robert and Joanna Seibert award. Joanna and her husband Robert have three grown children and six grandchildren and have lived in Little Rock for thirty-three years.

LaVergne, TN USA
22 October 2010

201865LV00003B/1/P